CHARLES DOWDING'S VEGETABLE COURSE

CHARLES DOWDING'S VEGETABLE COURSE

F

FRANCES LINCOLN LIMITED
PUBLISHERS

PAGE 2 Four varieties of beetroot: (left to right) 'Golden Detroit', 'Boltardy', 'Chioggia' and 'White'.
RIGHT Carrots pulled for a course lunch in June: 'Early Nantes', 'Purple Haze' and 'Rainbow Mixed'.

Frances Lincoln Limited
4 Torriano Mews
Torriano Avenue
London NW5 2RZ
www.franceslincoln.com

Charles Dowding's Vegetable Course
Copyright © Frances Lincoln Limited 2012
Text and photographs copyright © Charles Dowding 2012
Drawings copyright © Susie Dowding 2012
First Frances Lincoln edition 2012

A catalogue record for this book is available from the British Library.

ISBN 978-0-7112-3267-9

Printed and bound in China

2 3 4 5 6 7 8 9

Contents

INTRODUCTION

Teaching day courses in the gardens at Lower Farm has brought me into contact with many wonderful people, some of whom are new to gardening and some with a lifetime's experience.

They all share a desire to discover easier and more productive ways of managing their plots and gardens, to enjoy more food with richer flavours and over a longer season, and to gain a better idea of 'what happens next', enabling harvests to continue through all seasons.

Many course participants offer tips of their own, which reminds me how much there is still to learn, even after three decades of experimenting with vegetables and growing large quantities for sale. Yet there is also a surprisingly simple way of growing your own food, once you get the hang of not digging and of sowing seeds in exactly their right season. Start well, allow yourself to wonder and enjoy the journey: this is the essence of my course.

No-dig success

My own situation is unusual in spanning the gap between domestic and market gardening. Although I produce a lot of vegetables, I do not feel at home with machinery and have managed to scale upwards from a few raised beds, doing everything by hand as though still in a small garden.

Key to success has been a no-dig approach, saving the time of digging and also of much weeding, because *many fewer* weeds grow on undisturbed soil. Fellow growers and all gardeners who continually battle to keep on top of weeds are intrigued by my soil's cleanliness. Having fewer weeds means I can manage a larger garden and look after the soil more carefully.

Searching for a combination of economic viability and high quality of food has led me to try many ways of enhancing soil fertility. I find that growth and quality

Charles with trays of salad seedlings in autumn.

are improved by simply covering my beds with an inch or two of compost over their surface, which means two-thirds of the total area each year (paths and beds' sloping sides make up the other third).

Vegetables are hungry plants. Whatever their eventual size, we spend the same amount of time sowing, planting and weeding them, so it makes sense to maintain soil at a highly productive level.

Lower Farm gardens

The gardens are in three parts, started in 1997, 1999 and 2006 respectively. They cover an acre of undug beds whose output is vegetables and salads. I sell them locally, the salads as bags of mixed, washed leaves.

Outdoors the vegetables grow in the undug beds, with a northerly aspect, and there are also two polytunnels of 5.5×9m (18×30ft) and 3.5×18m (12×60ft), for tomatoes, basil, cucumber and melons in summer, and salad plants in winter and early spring.

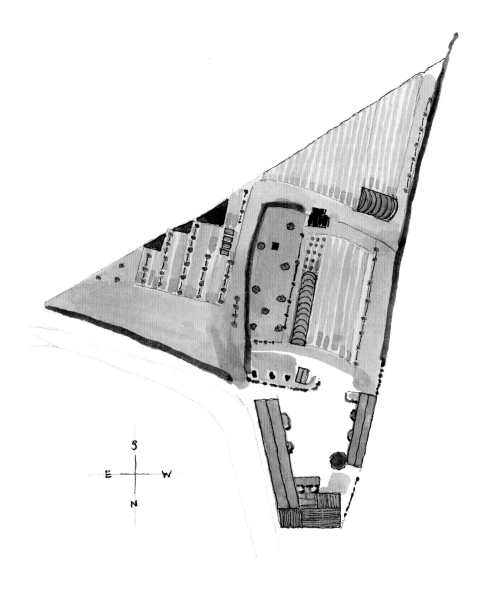

BOTTOM GARDEN We moved to Lower Farm in November 1997 and I was in a hurry to plant garlic and sow broad beans in the old kitchen garden, which was at the time a weedy paddock for goats.

Before year's end, I dug half of it, removing docks, dandelions and some couch grass, incorporating goat manure and shaping the upturned soil into 4ft (1.2m) wide beds with 0.5m (18in) pathways. The digging gave me immediate access to soil for sowing and planting.

Plants grew brilliantly in the dark soil, which had probably received a lot of manure and nightsoil over the centuries. Also growing in the first year were residual

LEFT Buildings and gardens at Lower Farm: orchard on left, bottom garden (with hen run) in the middle, top field above.

RIGHT Bottom Garden, August 2005, with asparagus on the left.

Top Field, September 2011 2010. From left: oriental leaves, leeks, chicories, beans, parsnips, cabbages.

grasses, which I removed with a trowel, and plenty of annual weeds, which I hoed. By the following year, because I was starting a small vegetable box scheme, I was looking for more ground.

TOP FIELD I cast my eye on the field above, growing organic wheat for a second year, and my brother agreed to relinquish the awkward triangle of its bottom corner, about a fifth of an acre. I hacked a hole through a hedge of brambles and found myself in a sticky morass of compacted clay.

The first job was digging out all the docks. There were strangely few annual weeds; maybe the soil was just too boggy, and it was a wet autumn. The surface layer was soft and sticky, after the passage in August of a spring tine cultivator. So I took the plunge and shaped two beds about 20m (65ft) long and slightly raised, by shovelling a shallow layer of soil from path to bed. Then I spread an inch of horse manure on top and sowed broad beans in November.

The soil felt like glue but the plants somehow grew, until succumbing in May to terrible chocolate spot, which resulted in few beans to eat. By now I had made beds on the whole plot and there were tiny onions, pencil-thin leeks and cabbages with no hearts. I hoed plenty of weed seedlings every two or three weeks, in soil that changed from sticky when wet to rock hard when dry.

There was a serious lack of air in this soil: it had been squashed out by the repeated passage of heavy machines. Unsure how long it would take to improve, I continued to mulch the beds with an inch or two of horse manure and green waste compost every autumn. In fact, during the second year

growth was almost normal, with significantly fewer weeds, and I felt encouraged.

When looking at the plot now, it is hard to believe such a history because growth is so abundant. In heavy rain, water soaks in instead of running off, unlike on the ploughed field above. Weed growth is minimal, harvests are high and plants are healthy.

ORCHARD In the autumn of 2005 I took over, unexpectedly, another triangular bottom corner of the same field, also damp and facing north. Its soil quality had been restored by six years of grass, so worms were busy – and the docks were even larger!

At the time I did not want any more land for growing, and mulled over how to manage it. In February 2006 I experimented with mulching the top corner, laying black plastic on the pasture plants, which included dandelion, couch grass and creeping buttercup. In late May I removed the mulch and spread 7–10cm (3–4in) of green waste compost on the mostly clean soil; then I

Espaliered apple trees in their fifth summer with a wealth of vegetables growing between them.

planted winter squash, and removed some remaining couch grass with a trowel, several times. The squash harvest was good.

My next decision was to plant fruit trees, mostly apples, in this whole plot, thinking to grow fruit without having to spend too much time there. Then in March 2007 I created between two rows a dig/no-dig experiment, which has become a valuable part of the gardens – to the point where I have had to dig out and transplant the neighbouring apple trees, whose roots were beginning to invade the experimental beds.

I have also been experimenting here with different materials for mulching the strips of pasture between rows of apple trees, to see which mulches work well and how long it is before vegetables can be planted into clean, undisturbed soil. Results have been mostly excellent and inform the advice I offer in this book.

On one of my courses in October 2008 I was fortunate to have participating Mike Bowser, who had grown apples commercially for many years. He spotted that I was actually using the space for vegetables as much as for fruit and advised me to convert the trees to espaliers, to make plenty of room for access between the rows, and I commenced that autumn, even though the trees had not been pruned with this in mind. They had many branches growing outwards and upwards, and needed careful re-training; and they look unconventional now. However, within two years the espalier training of more-or-less horizontal branches was achieved, in a homespun way, using string, hazel poles and bamboo canes. Although fruit growing is not covered in this book I urge you to give it a go, for using space on fences and in odd corners, to give more structure to your garden and considerable beauty at blossom and fruiting times. Follow common sense when pruning, according to the shapes you want – the possibilities are endless. And you can shape trees cheaply; there is no need for an expensive post-and-wire framework to grow fan-trained and espalier fruit.

Grow your ideas

This book is distilled from my experience of thirty bountiful years, at Lower Farm and elsewhere, during which I have tried out many ways of maintaining soil, sowing seed, controlling weeds, watering plants and harvesting produce. It is a concentrated summary of all my successes and failures. Mistakes have been a particularly useful, if painful, help in establishing the possibilities for achieving more abundant harvests.

The book is not an A to Z of vegetable growing: rather it aims to encourage and enlighten gardeners with the main knowledge needed to grow plenty of healthy vegetables. At the same time I hope I will show you that a well-tended plot of vegetables can be as beautiful and pleasurable as an ornamental garden. The great beauty of vegetables is not always applauded or even considered, but when well grown, in healthy soil, they have considerable allure. There is a rich palette of colours and shades and a fine range of shapes to choose from, and they can be grown in combinations that are eye-catching and uplifting when leaves are in sparkling health.

I hope you enjoy the book and find it helps you to grow more food on your plot, and achieve better harvests for less effort.

NEW WAYS TO GROW
SORTING THE NECESSARY FROM THE UNNECESSARY

The path this book will lead you down is partly different to that established by recent vegetable gardening lore, which has been influenced by historical trends and misunderstandings, about soil in particular. Also, much commonly offered advice is based on assumptions that are not stated – for example, that 'you need planks of wood when venturing on to wet soil in order to avoid compaction' includes an unspoken assumption that the soil has been dug or loosened in some way. Yet I garden on clay and push heavy wheelbarrows over it without causing compaction, because the undug soil has developed a firm structure. Most worries about compaction apply to dug soil, because digging damages structure. There are other key points that, despite their seeming unusual at first sight, I have found to be invaluable for success with vegetables.

Soil preparation simplified

The usual recommendation is to dig or even double dig the soil for growing vegetables. Because this is repeated so many times, most gardeners accept the task *without wondering if it is really necessary.*

In fact there is no need to dig at all, and my comparisons of growth on dug and undug soil in adjacent beds (see chapter 4) have revealed to me, and to many course participants and visitors, the temporary harm done by soil cultivation. The two undug beds grow more abundantly in spring, while the dug soil is recovering from being dug, before it catches up in autumn. The dug beds have more weeds and are less easy to water because their clay surface tends to smear and cap.

So my advice is simple: disturb your soil as little as possible, though sometimes you may have to, as when digging parsnips, planting trees and removing some large weeds. Initial clearance of weedy and grassy ground can mostly be achieved with mulches such as cardboard and compost, and some digging out of woody plants, as described in chapter 5. Thereafter, keep the surface clean by looking for weeds, and pulling or hoeing them at all times – a regular task that becomes easy once soil settles down to an undisturbed life.

Friends in the soil

Soil is alive with helpful bacteria, fungi, worms, beetles and so forth, which appreciate being fed with composted organic matter on a regular basis. I spread an inch or two on the surface of my beds every year, mostly as I clear plants in the late autumn. Surface compost weathers to a soft mulch over winter and can be directly sown or planted into.

Making and sourcing enough compost to spread on all beds every year is a worthwhile

Charles spreading home-made compost in October, on a bed just cleared of beans.

Spreading compost between rows of carrots in May.

aim, because it increases harvests and also the ease of gardening. Think of it as feeding the soil, rather than feeding plants. The insoluble nutrients in organic matter on top of undug soil become accessible to plants through a proliferation of mycorrhizal fungi, and the compost mulch conserves moisture.

Soil does not need to be mixed, stirred, scraped or tickled. Only large lumps of organic matter on top require some knocking around with a fork or rake in order to create an even surface, mostly in winter and spring.

Using compost

Compost is either plant matter or animal manure, or both, which has decomposed in the presence of some air to a dark brown, concentrated essence of soil life (see chapter 8). Preferably it has matured to become crumbly and soft, but it is still usable if sticky and wet; spreading it on the surface helps air to finish the decomposition process.

Compost fertilizes soil, but in a different way to man-made fertilizers, which are mostly water soluble and contain little or no organic matter. This makes them prone to being washed out of soil before plants can use all their nutrients. It means they must be applied carefully at specific times of year and in different quantities for different plants.

In contrast, compost's nutrients are nearly all water insoluble, remaining present but unavailable until a combination of suitable temperature and roots searching for food allows them to be taken up by plants.

Hence it is possible, and also most practical, to spread compost in autumn and winter without fear of nutrients being washed out. Low temperatures mean that soil life mostly hibernates, and plant food in the compost is held safely in readiness for the growing season to come.

Compost can even be spread where you are to sow carrots and parsnips. Common advice is not to, but this *assumes* it is being dug in, creating pockets of uneven fertility and a tendency for roots to fork. When spread on the surface, compost enriches soil slowly and evenly, which results in more abundant harvests of all vegetables, carrots and parsnips included. Sow seeds in the compost, to germinate and feed in it as well as rooting.

Clean soil in three stages

Weeds are a cause of aggravation to many gardeners, yet they can be made simpler to deal with than is often realized. Once soil is clean of most weed seeds, sowing and growing become easier and more enjoyable.

There are three stages to this, with the greatest effort needed in year one.

1. Clear the ground of existing woody plants. Either you can then mulch weeds, for different lengths of time according to which weeds are present; or you can clear them by hand, or even hoe them off if the soil is dry.
2. Pull or hoe all new weeds *when small*, long before they flower and create new seeds. It is far easier to pull out a small weed than a large one, and soil is then kept clear for your plants. Regrowth of

perennial weeds such as creeping grasses and bindweed needs regular removal with a trowel, with the aim of weakening roots so that, with one or two exceptions, they disappear completely.
3. Soil that is left undug and has some well-rotted organic matter spread on top is in a calm and fertile state which, in my experience, lessens the need for weeds to grow. The few that do are easier to remove.

Less feeding and watering

When growing in undisturbed, well-nourished soil, plants can access nutrients as needed. *No extra feeding of vegetables is necessary.* Only container-grown plants require regular feeding, as well as watering.

In open soil, watering plants in undug soil with a compost mulch on the surface is no more than an occasional job. New plants need watering in once or twice, and are then best left alone to send roots downward. Subsequent watering is most effective when done thoroughly and with long intervals between.

Exceptions, in sunny and warm weather, are salad plants making regular new leaves, fast-growing vegetables such as tomatoes and cucumbers, and shallow-rooting plants such as celery and lamb's lettuce.

A simpler way of rotating vegetables

A mantra of much gardening advice is the principle of four-yearly rotation. Although a sound idea, this is often impractical, especially in small plots, and can be discouraging, creating an obligation to grow a quarter of this and a quarter of that. Furthermore, a four-year rotation is almost impossible if in making full use of the soil you grow two harvests a year.

Instead, I advise simply that you *grow exactly what you want to eat*, with some planning before the season begins. Make a list – then look up when each vegetable needs to be sown, how much space it will

take up and how long it needs to grow. You will notice that many harvests occur in late spring and early summer, such as salads, spinach, carrots, early potatoes and garlic. After you have harvested these you can then sow or plant the free ground again for an autumn or winter harvest. There are lots of ideas for this in chapter 12.

In terms of rotating plants to minimize their exposure to pest and disease, I recommend simply keeping as long a time interval as you can between vegetables of the same families (see page 141), because of their potential vulnerability to the same problems.

This results in 'rotations' of different lengths. For instance, in my gardens, where I grow a lot of salad, there are sometimes only two years between crops of the lettuce family, compared with about four years between vegetables of the onion family (alliums) and ten years between potatoes. The gaps change in length as I grow more or less of certain vegetables every year.

Carrots from undug clay: (left to right) 'Early Nantes', 'Purple Haze' 'Rainbow' and more 'Early Nantes'.

Green and brown manures

Green manures are plants grown for their nutrients and organic matter to be added back to the soil, but they need skill to manage and several disadvantages are rarely addressed, especially for small plots. Before sowing, consider three things:

- They mostly need digging in, and then *require time* to decompose in the soil, and there is a tendency for nutrients in soil to be used for this decomposition process in preference to meeting the needs of growing plants.

- Green manures are often presented as an 'easy option': sow the seed and walk away, knowing that fertility is improving. In fact if you do this, weeds will also grow and set seed, lining you up for extra weeding in the following season. Green manures are therefore best weeded as they grow. (I say more about this in chapter 6.) Also, both while they are growing and decomposing, slugs often breed in the damp soil and decaying green matter.

- While green manures are growing, you have foregone the chance of growing or overwintering more vegetables.

Instead of a green manure, I suggest you build fertility with compost and concentrate it in a smaller, well-managed area, cropped all the time as space becomes free. For example, you can sow carrots after lettuce or plant purple sprouting broccoli and kale after a garlic harvest, or French beans after an early beetroot harvest, or spring cabbage after runner beans, and so on.

If your garden has more space than you need, rather than sowing a green manure I suggest you plant some fruit bushes and trees, and concentrate the vegetables in a smaller plot.

Companion planting – not so simple

There are benefits of close relationships among particular plants. Long ago I witnessed the extra growth of Brussels sprout plants with some lettuce planted between

Spring flowers: broad beans and lupins. The lupins are perennial and for ornament.

them, compared to the slower growth of those with empty soil between. I offer a number of successful plant combinations in chapter 12.

However, companion planting is sometimes misrepresented as a panacea for most ills. I have found no companionable answers to many pest problems. It is not that they don't work, but the effects are mostly small and incomplete. My vegetables have suffered damage when supposedly protected by companions, as with onions against carrot fly, marigolds against aphids and carrots against leek moth. I still grow beautiful marigolds with tomatoes, just without any expectation that all pests will disappear.

Health in the garden

Healthy plants have a beautiful bloom and their harvests are more nutritious and long lived than those of unhealthy plants. That was the answer I gave the chef in a restaurant I supply who asked why my basil leaves keep healthy for so much longer than other basil he bought.

Successful gardening happens when one concentrates on *health* rather than disease. An analysis of healthy soil might find all sorts of bacteria *we* are uncomfortable with, but they belong in the soil, and the point is that they help plants to grow healthily.

It is strange that the case for hospital-style hygiene is presented as important in the garden – for instance in recommendations to wash and even sterilize all pots and trays before re-use, and disinfect the greenhouse, as though your plants are vulnerable to all sorts of unseen diseases.

The healthy plants in my garden are raised in pots and trays which have seen decades

of use, more than once a year, without ever being washed, rinsed or even brushed out. I simply wipe the greenhouse and tunnels with cold water in the winter, to keep the glass and polythene clear and allow light in.

Animal manures do wonders for soil and are ready to use after a year or so in a heap; they certainly do not need to rot under cover for several years as I recently read. I also heard a permaculturist say, with a straight face, that mulches help prevent soil bacteria from contaminating the undersides of plants' leaves when it rains heavily!

Soil is full of hard-working, useful bacteria, fungi and nematodes: wonderful growth happens when we understand and encourage the organisms that encourage soil and plant health. Disease-causing organisms may also be present in healthy soil, but they can only take hold when health is absent, or when plants are dying off at the end of their growing cycle, at which point disease is a necessary part of the recycling process.

Be adventurous and nurture the garden

I really hope that, through understanding and adapting the advice I give in this book, you feel able within a short space of time to turn your plot into *your* space, using methods you are comfortable with, to grow what *you* want.

To enjoy harvests of healthy vegetables I suggest you garden with the ones applicable to you and your plot, starting with a good look at the next chapter, to gain a clear idea of what needs doing when.

A vibrant selection of June vegetables: lettuce, asparagus, garlic, carrot, calabrese, broad beans and potatoes.

TAKING YOU THROUGH A YEAR

KNOWING WHAT NEEDS DOING WHEN

Gardening feels more fulfilling when the jobs that need doing are spread throughout the year and at the most effective time. 'Little and often' has three marvellous results:

- It becomes easier to keep on top of growth at peak times, when you can otherwise feel overwhelmed by many jobs arising as plants need tending, harvests are happening, weeds are growing and seeds want sowing.
- You spend less time overall, because jobs are completed more quickly when tackled at the right moment. This particularly applies to weeding, when you save much time through dealing with small weeds instead of large ones.
- The plot and garden look tidier and more beautiful, with an abundance of healthy growth.

To help you achieve this happy state, I will take you through a year of vegetable growing, covering the most important seasonal tasks, after explaining some important jobs that keep cropping up.

LEFT New year: using a rake to break surface lumps of compost in January.
BELOW Kale growing in the orchard under a snow-covered net in February 2009.

Terms defined

CLEARING means removing all leaves and stems of a harvested vegetable, and all weeds. The small, fine roots of vegetables and annual weeds can be left in soil. Only some perennial weeds need all their roots removing (see chapter 6).

COMPOST is well-decomposed organic matter, either from the garden or brought in as animal manure and other composts.

HARVESTING ranges from regular pickings of salad leaves, courgettes and tomatoes off the same plants for many months, to pulling potatoes or onions in one harvest and clearing ground at the same time. Weather may sometimes change the harvesting possibilities.

INDOORS means a greenhouse, polytunnel, conservatory, windowsill and any other place sheltered from rain and cold. Everywhere else is outdoors!

PLANTING means the setting out of growing plants and happens at different times to sowing; for example, leeks are sown in April and planted in June or July. *I am specific in the use of these two words and I do not say 'plant' when I mean 'sow'!* Planting also describes the setting out of large seeds and tubers such as potatoes and small plants such as onion sets and garlic. Unless otherwise stated, planting is outdoors.

PREPARING GROUND is a combination of *clearing*, so that you have bare soil with no weeds, followed by *composting* if none has been applied for a year or more, and possibly (not always) some raking to knock out lumps of the surface compost. The time between spreading compost and planting varies from ten minutes in

Sowing radish between tatsoi and pak choi in my polytunnel in February.

summer, when a harvest has finished and new plants are waiting to go in, to six months in winter, when soil is composted after autumn harvests and may lie empty until spring.

RAKING/FORKING means lateral movement of either tool through the surface organic matter, after it has weathered for a month or so, to knock any lumps open and develop a soft tilth over all the soil.

SOWING means the placing of seeds in drills and holes in the soil outdoors, or in compost in trays and pots indoors. I give detailed advice on sowing methods and timings in chapters 10–12.

WATERING may be with a hose or can. If it is dry, I suggest a good soak every week rather than a sprinkling every day; checking with a trowel, to see how far down the applied moisture has travelled, will help you know how much water to give.

WEEDING applies to all unwanted plants, which may be either hoed and left *in situ*, when weeds are small and soil is dry, or removed by hand to a bucket, perhaps using a trowel.

January and February

January and February are quiet months, and how much needs doing depends on what you achieved in autumn. It should be possible to harvest plants such as leeks and parsnips in undug soil with a mulch of compost, which freezes less hard than dug soil.

PREPARING GROUND

  COMPOSTING Spread well-rotted compost or manure on any bare soil, thus allowing time for frost to soften the organic matter.

  RAKING/FORKING In less cold and drier weather, to break open the larger lumps of surface manure and compost which were spread in autumn.

SOWING Although it is possible for a few vegetables, there is little to be gained from sowing seeds outdoors now, although garlic can be planted if you have not already done so. You can make indoor sowings of lettuce, spinach, onion, cabbage, cauliflower and broad bean; parsley, dill and broad beans too outdoors too after mid-February, and parsnips if it is dry enough.

HARVESTING Roots such as parsnip and swede can be lifted, leeks too. If birds and animals can be kept at bay, there can be kale, Brussels sprouts, and cabbages such as 'Tundra' and 'January King'. In milder weather, especially in February, it should be possible to harvest a few salad leaves under cover and some lamb's lettuce outside.

Salad leaves in February from my polytunnel.

March

PREPARING GROUND

  WEEDING Already there will be grasses, chickweed, bittercress to pull, and a trowel is useful for removing roots of dandelion, couch grass and other perennials which will now be revealing themselves. In a dry spring, hoeing the seedlings of annual weeds is worthwhile.

  COMPOSTING As for January.

  RAKING/FORKING As for January and aiming for smaller lumps.

SOWING Indoors as for February and also tomato, chilli, aubergine, pepper, melon (all with some extra warmth), pea, calabrese, celery, celeriac, beetroot; outdoors parsnip, onion, radish.

PLANTING Garlic in early March, early potato, onion sets, shallots, broad beans and asparagus crowns after mid-month.

HARVESTING As for February but with many more salad leaves and spinach indoors; purple sprouting broccoli and some rhubarb outdoors.

April

PREPARING GROUND

CLEARING Of leek trimmings, winter cabbage and Brussels sprout stalks, flowering winter salad plants.

WEEDING General hoeing of weed seedlings is possible whenever soil is reasonably dry; continue removing perennials.

COMPOSTING Assuming the rest of your plot is already composted, new compost is needed only where ground has just been cleared, for instance after harvesting leeks and Brussels sprouts.

RAKING/FORKING As for January unless you have a reasonably fine tilth already.

SOWING Similar to March indoors, adding courgettes, squash, cucumber, basil around mid-month; also leeks, carrots and beetroot outdoors. But avoid sowing all your seed – wait until May and June to sow summer beans and winter brassicas.

PLANTING Potatoes of all kinds, calabrese, cauliflower, beetroot, globe artichoke, pea, beetroot, lettuce, broad beans, onions, spinach.

WATERING Under cloches of overwintered salads.

HARVESTING The final leeks, savoy cabbages and purple sprouting; asparagus by month's end; plenty of salad leaves indoors, but plants may also be flowering and many finish cropping by late April.

May

PREPARING GROUND

CLEARING Of last overwintered kale, purple sprouting, chard, spinach and overwintered salads.

WEEDING Many weeds grow fast in May, so you will find yourself hoeing, hand weeding and also cutting or pulling grass along plot edges; be vigilant about weeds from now on, as their speed of growth in warmer weather can easily result in a plot being 'taken over' and you then become discouraged, whereas dealing with them when small is easier and encourages good morale.

COMPOSTING After any clearing, where the soil has no compost residue on the surface, and to 'earth up' potatoes.

SOWING INDOORS OR OUTDOORS Brussels sprouts, autumn cabbage and sweetcorn; then wait until mid-month to sow runner and French beans and cucumber indoors, or early June outdoors.

PLANTING Indoor plants such as tomatoes and aubergines can be planted; courgettes, squashes, celery and celeriac can be planted outdoors as long as all risk of frost has passed.

WATERING Mainly for plants newly set out and for salad plants.

HARVESTING Only salad leaves, spinach, radish, asparagus, rhubarb, overwintered cabbage and salad onion: now is the time known as the hungry gap.

June

PREPARING GROUND

CLEARING Only a little of this in June, after spinach, overwintered cabbage and onion and a few salad plants.

WEEDING As for May; keep the soil clean around all plants and also where sowing or planting is yet to happen.

SOWING INDOORS OR OUTDOORS
Sow kale, purple sprouting, savoy cabbage, swede and a second batch of lettuce in early June; around or after mid-month is good for winter carrots and beetroot, also bulb fennel and autumn calabrese.

PLANTING Brussels sprouts, all kinds of summer beans, outdoor cucumber and tomato in early June; setting out leek and swede plants by month's end will give them time to grow large.

WATERING As for May.

HARVESTING An exciting month, as the first harvests of beetroot, carrots, potatoes, courgette, calabrese, cauliflower, lettuce hearts, broad beans and peas can all come ready at different moments, and asparagus continues until the last week.

A June harvest of broad beans, asparagus, spinach, cabbage and beetroot.

July

PREPARING GROUND

CLEARING Already there will be harvests finishing, such as salads, carrot, beetroot, spinach, peas, overwintered broad beans, garlic, shallots. As soon as the last picking is done, clear all debris and weeds (there should be few weeds) and firm soil with feet – gently if wet, with full weight if dry – and then plant straight away with plants you have raised or bought.

WEEDING In dry summers there may be fewer weeds, but keep your eyes open because a few weeds setting seed causes much more work for years to come; also have a search for weeds under large leaves of courgettes, beans and brassicas.

COMPOSTING Spread 1cm (½in) only on soil which has none left on top, either before new sowings and plantings or, later, around plants that are already growing.

SOWING INDOORS OR OUTDOORS Sow
lettuce for autumn, other autumn/winter salads such as endive and chicory, and parsley to overwinter.

PLANTING Kale, swede, savoy cabbage, cauliflower, purple sprouting, beetroot in early July; also bulb fennel and calabrese.

WATERING In dry weather most value comes from watering salads and all larger plants that are flowering and cropping, such as beans and courgettes.

HARVESTING July is an abundant time after June's hint of summer feasts: potatoes, peas, broad beans and courgettes may be especially fruitful, globe artichokes come ready and garlic wants lifting by early July, to dry and be stored; also shallots.

August

PREPARING GROUND

CLEARING Continue removing any crop residues so as to sow or plant again, often on the same day – for example, sow turnips after clearing onions, or sow land cress after early French beans have finished.

WEEDING As for July.

COMPOSTING Possibly before planting autumn salads.

SOWING INDOORS OR OUTDOORS
Oriental leaves, rocket, coriander and chervil are best sown in early August, also spinach and chard to overwinter; then land cress and winter purslane mid-month, followed by overwintering cabbage, onions and lettuce in the last week; also lamb's lettuce at month's end, for harvesting from November, and salads for planting in September to grow under a cloche through winter.

PLANTING Chicory for radicchio in early August, endive, rocket, oriental leaves, chervil, coriander, spinach, chard.

WATERING As for July; well-composted soil needs less water than usual, and you can save water when sowing seeds in dry soil by watering only the bottom of the drill you have drawn out, so that seeds fall on moist soil but are then covered with dry soil.

HARVESTING A season of gluts is possible, of runner and French beans, tomatoes, courgettes, cucumber; also onions and potatoes to store.

August often brings an abundance of cherry tomatoes – 'Sungold', 'Sakura', 'Rosada', et al.

September

PREPARING GROUND

CLEARING As soon as possible after any final harvests, remove all stems and leaves of vegetables that finish to make way for a final sowing of lamb's lettuce and plantings of salads such as oriental leaves.

WEEDING As for July.

COMPOSTING Compost may be spread where vegetables have finished and the ground is not needed for second sowings; and/or oriental leaves can be sown as an edible green manure.

SOWING INDOORS OR OUTDOORS In
the first week, a final sowing of lamb's lettuce, mizuna, rocket, mustards, leaf radish; also for lettuce and endive to overwinter indoors, followed by mid-month, indoor sowings of all other winter salads for indoor leaves.

PLANTING Salads for late autumn and for later covering with a cloche, spinach and then cabbage, onions, lettuce to overwinter in September's second half.

WATERING Many summer vegetables such as beans, tomatoes and courgettes will now be winding down and need little more water, so this is a good month (if dry) to water celeriac, leeks and other autumn or winter vegetables which will be bulking up in any warm autumn weather.

HARVESTING Often the most abundant month, with an overlap of summer and autumn harvests, meaning a plethora of choices over what to eat.

October

PREPARING GROUND

CLEARING Many vegetables finish in October, including courgette and squash plants, summer beans, lettuce, sweetcorn, tomato, cucumber, aubergine, pepper. Remove all weeds as you clear and cut all cleared vegetable stems to 15cm (6in) length before composting them.

WEEDING Weeds will be losing vigour, including bindweed, but grasses and chickweed can still flower and set seed, so pull any you see, by hand, as soil is usually too damp for hoeing in October.

COMPOSTING You can spread compost and manure as soon as ground is cleared; or if planting garlic and broad beans, you can dib them in first and then spread compost or manure on top of the cloves and bean seeds.

SOWING/PLANTING Garlic cloves are best planted in early October and broad bean seeds at month's end or in early November, the vegetable year's final sowing; also plant salads under cover by mid-October if possible, so that plants have time to root properly before winter.

WATERING Needed for dry soil under cover after pulling out summer vegetables such as tomatoes. Be sure to water thoroughly, often for longer than you would imagine, to be sure of the soil being moist before you plant winter vegetables.

HARVESTING Another month of abundance even though many summer vegetables have finished, replaced by parsnip, celeriac, cabbage, leek, Brussels sprouts and squash.

October harvests boast an overlap of summer and winter vegetables.

November

PREPARING GROUND

CLEARING Larger stems and leaves, including asparagus, are best cleared to a compost heap but smaller debris such as parsnip, leek and endive leaves can be left *in situ* and covered with compost as soon as harvests have been taken.

WEEDING If you have kept on top of weeds through the spring, summer and autumn there should be very few to deal with, but keep tweaking out any small grasses, cleavers, dandelions, etc.

COMPOSTING Continue as before so that more and more of the plot is covered as harvests finish, and you can also spread compost around growing plants such as kale.

HARVESTING Fresh harvests include spinach, chard, the last calabrese, parsnip, swede, leeks, salad leaves (including pak choi, tatsoi, mustards, rocket, chervil, endive, chicory, spinach), carrot, beetroot, celeriac, turnip – and the last four can now be harvested to store, especially if hard frost is forecast.

December

PREPARING GROUND – CLEARING, WEEDING, COMPOSTING Similar

to November, meaning that most of the plot is clear and composted by Christmas, with the rest of the ground growing harvests for winter.

HARVESTING Brussels sprouts, savoy cabbage, kale, leeks, parsnip, swede, chicory roots for forcing, salads such as lamb's lettuce, land cress and winter purslane; also stored endive and radicchio and some leaves from plants under cover.

TOOLS AND EQUIPMENT
A FEW HELPERS YOU REALLY NEED

Gardening involves the repeated use of a few simple tools, so buy the best you can afford, or look out for well-crafted old ones. See also Suppliers and Resources on page 200.

Much of what is deemed necessary for gardening is really in the category of gadgets or luxuries, and I want this chapter to save you money by highlighting the tools and accessories you *really* need.

Tools

My favourite tools are made of copper, or to be precise they are 95 per cent copper and 5 per cent tin, as used by the Roman army for their swords: the metal is strong, not magnetic, and does not rust. This is a keen advantage for trowels, hoes and spades where smooth, sharp blades make for effortless use, and there is no need for any regular cleaning or oiling to protect the metal.

Although the copper alloy is a little less hard than iron, and might suffer in soils with flint or large amounts of stone, the tools are designed to endure. I have found copper trowels last better than ones made of hard stainless steel, which often snap after a year or two, at a weak point near the handle.

◀ Dibber

Dibbers are invaluable for making holes of about the same size as root balls of plants grown in plugs and modules, onion sets, garlic cloves and even potato tubers at planting out time. You can dib holes quickly and then fill them with whatever you are planting, including larger seeds such as peas and beans.

The dibbers I recommend are spade handles with a pointed end, usually in wood. Most dibbers are too short to offer much leverage and also it is difficult to create a pattern of planting holes with so little perspective.

You can make your own quite easily, starting with a wooden handle about 75cm (30in) long: chisel the end and then sand it to make a rounded and pointed end for pushing into soil.

OPPOSITE Unlike the copper trowel above, the stainless-steel trowel below has a weak point where its thin shaft meets the blade.

◀ Bucket

A humble accessory, with many uses, from collecting weeds, crop residues and slugs to carrying water and bringing home harvests. Have a couple to hand.

◀ Garden fork (left)

Shorter and fatter prongs than a manure fork mean better durability for jobs like digging out plants, including parsnips, and for removing perennial weeds such as couch grass. Look for a sturdy handle that won't snap at the first hint of something firm.

▲ Manure fork (right)

Useful for turning and spreading compost and organic matter generally. Long, thin prongs make it too weak for any kind of digging work.

◀ Hoe

A good hoe has a thin blade with a sharp edge and slides easily through soil. The aim is to cut through all roots of small weeds at a shallow level, without bringing up lumps of soil in which they might survive before withering. Hoes come in many forms: Dutch hoes, draw hoes, onion hoes and swivel hoes, all with blades of varied size and at different angles. I recommend trying a few to see which you like, because everybody has a favourite type. I use a copper swivel hoe: its thin, sharp blade cuts cleanly when both pushing and pulling.

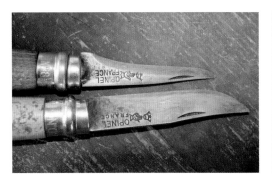

▲ Pocket knife

A small knife is often needed in the garden, for cutting string, sticks and flowers, trimming leeks, cabbages and tomato plants, deadheading and many of the other jobs that catch one's eye unexpectedly. It is a good habit to carry one in the pocket.

▲ Rake

Rakes are handy before sowing seeds, to knock lumps apart and create a smoother tilth, and to fill drills after sowing; also for collecting up surface debris such as leaves and grass. A standard short-pronged version has more uses than long-pronged rakes.

▲ Scythe

Scythes are more effective and adaptable than is often realized, especially when blades are not too long, say 60cm (24in). We use ours to trim grassy edges and for occasional cutting of nettles and brambles. Scything takes some practice but using a short blade helps, and it means you spare your neighbours (and yourself) the noise of a strimmer, although you may need a lawnmower for large areas of grass.

▲ Spade

Even in a no-dig garden, spades have many uses – making holes for trees and large plants, shaping beds, chopping waste matter, digging parsnips. A sharp end is invaluable: see the tips on sharpening on page 37. Copper or stainless-steel spades are worth the extra money, for they are much easier to use, because less soil sticks to them.

◀ Trowel

I use a trowel more than any other tool, for clearing ground, removing perennial weeds and making holes to plant tomatoes, courgettes, potatoes and so forth. Copper trowels are the easiest to use: they retain a sharp edge and slide easily through soil.

◀ Watering can

In dry periods a watering can is vital. Choose as large a can as is comfortable to hold when full. Also you will use a can frequently when propagating plants, for which a smaller one with a fine rose is useful.

Wheelbarrow

Ranking with the bicycle as a supremely cost-effective, energy-efficient and useful invention, a wheelbarrow carries all kinds of materials, to and from the compost heap above all.

Accessories

Some of these accessories will appeal and some will be inappropriate for your plot. Many are cheap for the benefits they bring: fleece, for example, is easy to use and extremely cost effective. Structures such as polytunnels may seem daunting to erect and maintain, but they offer wonderful new ways of achieving better harvests.

Cloche

A simple and effective way to grow salads in winter, and to warm air and soil in spring. Covering hoops with polythene affords most warmth to plants but means some ventilation and watering is often needed. Alternatively you can lay fleece or mesh over cloche hoops (see below), ensuring good ventilation, or directly on plants, which is even simpler and quicker.

Cloche hoops

You can save much money by making cloche hoops out of materials such as alkathene water pipe, electrical conduit or wire. They can be up to 1.2m (4ft) wide, to cover whole beds, but wider cloches are also taller, so they need to be strong, according to average wind speeds. Push hoops 10–15cm (4–6in) into the soil and space them about 1m (39in) apart. You can then stretch covers tightly over them and weight them down along the edges with bricks or with bought pegs.

Cold frame

A useful way of starting seedlings and for protecting tender plants, but the edges may harbour slugs: glass-sided frames, although more fragile, are best for slug-free growth.

Compost bins

Wooden sides and simple enclosures of old pallets or the cheapest conical plastic bins are effective: see chapter 8.

Containers for growing

Use anything that can hold compost and has a drainage hole at the bottom. Larger containers give harvests over a longer period, although it is possible to feed the compost of smaller pots and seed trays, which otherwise run low on nutrients.

Old pots are fine, but terracotta ones need more water than plastic. There is no need to wash out ones that you are re-using. You can also grow in boxes or crates that have been used for packing food, such as plastic mushroom boxes and polystyrene fish boxes: shopkeepers are often glad to give them away. Boxes with many holes can be lined with two or three sheets of newspaper.

Fleece and mesh

Both fleece and mesh should be re-usable many times over and for weather protection a few holes do not matter. Fleece is warmer than mesh and is most valuable in spring, for covering young plants against cold winds. You can also use it as a pest barrier in summer and autumn, and for frost protection in winter, when thicker grades or double layers are effective.

Mesh is cooler and stronger than fleece, and particularly useful in summer and autumn for protecting plants from brassica pests, carrot root flies and leek moths. Mesh comes with different-sized holes, and for protection against aphids and midges you need the finest grade.

These covers can be laid directly on plants, held firm at their edges with a weight

Fleece as frost and rabbit protection on radicchios in October 2010.

every 1m (39in) or so. They are light and flexible enough for leaves to push them up in growing, and plants thrive in the calm but airy environment underneath.

Greenhouse

Any walk-in structure allows you to do a lot of gardening when it is wet and windy; if you have enough space and money, a greenhouse can prove invaluable. Although expensive, glasshouses admit more light and retain more heat than polythene structures. and are excellent for raising plants, protecting crops in all seasons, keeping tools dry and so forth: I strongly recommend one if you can afford it. Otherwise a small polytunnel is cheaper (see page 36), as are lean-to plastic shelters for placing beside a house wall. I suggest some

kind of wooden staging if you use any of these structures for raising plants.

Where space for a structure is limited, you could use a portable 'mini-greenhouse' on wheels, often sold as a kit with shelving included. I would recommend one of these ahead of a cold frame, which takes up extra room and is all at ground level, and therefore cooler and with more risk of slug damage.

Netting

If pigeons, deer and rabbits are a pest, you will need some netting. Mesh size can be as much as 2.5cm (1in) and I find a 4m (13ft) wide roll of heavy-duty black netting is useful for many vegetables: its flexible diamond-shaped mesh allows for stretching to fit different widths of beds or rows, held up by sticks or cloche hoops, and it can be re-used for many years.

Polytunnel

Polytunnels are much less expensive than greenhouses and come in an infinite range of widths and lengths. Once you have succeeded with some outdoor vegetables, a polytunnel is a highly worthwhile next step for growing tender and out-of-season vegetables, indoor propagation of small plants, and also drying onions and garlic, and as a general storage space. Their polythene needs replacing every five to seven years.

Propagating trays

For indoor sowing and potting on, a whole range of products can be bought,

or retrieved at no cost, and re-used many times. Although it is unnecessary to clean or sterilize old pots and trays, most retail outlets feel obliged to use new ones and discard many once-used ones which are perfectly good for raising plants at home. You can also use egg boxes, yoghurt pots or any container of a suitable size, as long as it has either a porous bottom or a hole for excess water to drain out: no plants grow well in waterlogged compost.

Seed trays have no partition and are simple to use; I suggest using trays of 15 × 22cm (6 × 9in). Moving plants out of them involves some root disturbance, however.

I find that module trays (also called cell or plug trays) of hard plastic are good both in the sense that you can push each plant

These salads in the polytunnel in March were frozen many times in winter.

Filling a sixty-hole module tray with potting compost.

out with minimal damage to the root ball, and that you can re-use the trays time and again. Polystyrene trays are equally good but more expensive. The standard size is 35 × 22cm (14 × 9in) and may contain 24, 40 or 60 individual holes. The latter are good for growing salad plants, while 40-hole trays are good for brassicas (cabbage family), which benefit from a little more compost. Module trays may be difficult to find or buy: check my recommendations in Suppliers and Resources (page 200) and avoid trays in flimsy plastic such as 'inserts'.

For details of indoor sowing, see chapter 10.

Shed

You will need some kind of solid shelter for tools and equipment, and also for storing onions, garlic and other harvested vegetables. Few sheds give protection against frost, however, so a shed is not suitable for keeping potatoes and squash through winter.

Stone for sharpening

A simple stone is invaluable for running smoothly along the blade of spades and edgers, perhaps only twice a year. The aim is to remove jagged edges as much as to sharpen the blade, so it is not a highly skilled operation. But with some practice you may acquire a highly useful skill, and be able to sharpen a pocket knife too.

Water butt

A water butt is invaluable if there are ways to fill and refill it, especially for watering recently moved plants. Plastic butts of 100–200 litres may have lids and taps, but their water becomes smelly over time, from lack of oxygen, and occasional draining out and brushing of the inside is worthwhile.

EXPLAINING NO-DIG

REVELATIONS FROM AN EXPERIMENT

There are mysteries in soil, more than we may care to admit. Some are being highlighted by the experiment I have run since 2007, in which to understand more about the effect on soil of digging and not digging I compare growth of the same vegetables growing side by side in dug and undug beds.

I have found that harvests are as high, sometimes higher, in the absence of cultivation, while some extra quality of growth on undug soil may be apparent. Soil in the undug beds, with compost on its surface, is well drained, retains more moisture in dry springs, and grows fewer weeds and stronger vegetables, especially at the start of every season.

A key point is that *undug soil is firm*. This is a desirable state and not at all the same as compacted soil. Roots have freedom to travel, at the same time as being well anchored. As on a lawn, I can walk on my undug soil without compacting it because there is a strong matrix of holes, created by soil organisms and roots, all glued in place by organic matter.

Fertility is enhanced by an increase of undisturbed soil life, which mobilizes nutrients and helps plant roots to access them. This is most noticeable in early spring, when growth on undug soil is generally faster by comparison with dug soil, whose fertility, in terms of soil life, is still recovering from the winter digging.

A dig/no dig experiment

Setting up the experiment

Starting in March 2007, I marked out an area of old pasture, on heavy clay loam, with canes at the corners of four plots. Between the canes I ran string along the sides and ends of the beds. Then I scraped turves off the pathways all around, about 10cm (4in) or so thick, and placed them in the bed areas.

The sides and ends of the beds are of 2.5cm (1in) softwood planks, which I treated with a natural oil, OSMO wood protector. The planks are 22.5cm (9in) deep

The same vegetables growing in an undug bed in front and a dug bed behind.

and enclose beds of 1.5 × 2.5m (5 × 8½ft), with 45cm (18in) pathways between.

I filled the two undug beds with 20cm (8in) compost, which I placed on top of the grass, dandelions and buttercups. One-third of this was well-rotted horse manure as a first layer; then I used green waste compost for the remaining two-thirds and 10kg of rockdust. All sowing and planting on the undug beds is into the surface compost.

I created the two dug beds by first lifting turves off the pasture, and then placing the same ingredients as in the undug beds in the holes created, finally putting the upside-down turves on top. Sowing and planting in the first spring would have been easier if digging had happened in autumn or winter, to make the dug bed's soil easier to de-clod.

Running the experiment

I feed and crop the four beds as two pairs, giving each pair the same ingredients, except that I either put compost and/or manure on top (undug) or incorporate them (dug). I re-dig the dug beds every December, when I give both beds a barrowload of either home-made compost or well-rotted animal manure, equivalent to about a 5cm (2in) layer.

I sow or plant each pair of beds with identical crops and I replace any eaten plants and sowings to equalize the harvests aspect of the experiment; failed sowings, fortunately, are rare. I make all pairs of harvests at the same time, weighing and recording them, together with any observations on differences in quality.

The four experimental beds: from front, undug-dug-undug-dug.

Harvests from the experiment

Yields in both beds have been excellent, thanks to timely planting and replanting, good amounts of organic matter and a moisture-retentive clay soil. Over a whole season, each bed produces about 30kg vegetables, after unusable leaves, roots and pods have been graded out. The table opposite shows harvests of four years (2007–10), comparing those of dug and undug beds.

The differences between early and late harvests show how the no-dig beds start growing more quickly in spring, and the dug beds catch up in late summer and autumn.

Differences between growth

Discrepancies in growth on dug and undug beds are most apparent between March and June, when the dug soil, it seems,

VEGETABLE	HARVEST FROM DUG BEDS kg	HARVEST FROM UNDUG BEDS kg
Beans, dwarf 4 years	4.49	4.38
Beetroot 4 years	9.52	10.51*
Cabbage, red 3 years	8.77	5.75
Calabrese 1 year	1.12	0.62
Carrot 3 years	11.99	12.49
Celeriac 3 years	12.24	15.82
Chard 2 years	12.33	11.59*
Endive and chicory 3 years	11.76	14.42
Kale 1 year	3.95	4.02
Leek 4 years	12.05	13.25
Lettuce 4 years	29.11	33.25*
Onion 4 years	19.51	23.53*
Peas 4 years	23.51	24.12*
Parsnip 3 years	32.26	32.21
Potatoes, early 3 years	7.81	8.14*
Radish 3 years	1.59	2.03*
Salads, autumn 2 years	4.03	4.13
Spinach 3 years	16.43	21.36*
Turnip 2 years	11.97	9.54
TOTAL	234.44	251.16
Early harvests*	119.81	134.53
Late harvests**	114.63	116.63

* Early harvests are from April to early August and include beetroot, lettuce, onion, peas, potatoes, radish and spinach.

** Late harvests are all other vegetables listed here.

is recovering from being turned over and broken up. During spring and early summer, many vegetables on the dug beds, especially radish, onions and spinach, start growing more slowly. I also notice when comparing harvests of early season growth that in the undug beds the leaves of spinach and lettuce are thicker and glossier, the radish roots are more shiny and the onions have a deeper colour.

Then from about July there is a change as growth on the dug soil speeds up: celeriac

Potato harvest, May 2011, from the dug bed.

Potato harvest, May 2011, from the undug bed.

on the dug beds, for instance, which is smaller in June, suddenly grows faster from July, and by October has more or less caught up with celeriac on the undug soil. Summer-planted brassicas sometimes yield better on the dug beds.

The grand total of harvests over a whole season usually shows quite similar results, as the table shows. Many people's reaction on my courses in late summer and autumn, as they survey the similar-looking vegetables, is simply: 'Why bother digging if it does not increase growth?'

Differences between surfaces

It is fascinating to compare the smooth, brown clay of the dug soil with the fluffy, darker compost of the undug.

When watering in dry spells, I am struck by how easily the fast-flowing hose water soaks into the undug beds, being absorbed by the surface compost and then passing downwards through the unbroken capillary channels of the soil below. By contrast on the dug beds the water tends to cause a smearing of clay and then runs downhill

before it can all soak in, so I have to apply it in short bursts.

One might have thought that digging would open up soil and allow water to flow through. But before that can happen, it has to pass through a surface that has lost its structure. Thankfully I find that by late summer it is easier to water the dug soil, which suggests that soil organisms have, by then, restructured their home.

The dug bed's surface (right) cracks in dry April weather.

Differences in weed germination

More weeds germinate on the dug beds, most noticeably in early spring, many from seeds that have been in the soil a long time and brought to the surface by digging. I hoe shallowly in April and hand weed thereafter – only a little, because the soil is then clean, thanks to new weeds not being allowed to seed.

The compost I use is reasonably clean of weed seeds, meaning that only a few germinate on the undug beds in spring. If you use compost with many weed seeds, more weeding will be needed, but weeds should be easy to dislodge or to remove if larger.

There are no perennial weeds in any of the experimental beds because the original docks, dandelion and couch grass have been either dug out or turned over deeply in the dug beds, and smothered in the undug beds, where I removed a few weakened survivors with a trowel.

Differences in pests

The wooden sides of both beds are good for demarcating the experiment but are also, unfortunately, a habitat for slugs. On the whole I notice more slug damage on the dug beds, where I need to replace a few more plants every season than on the undug beds. Slugs appear to prefer a surface of dug clay to slither over, compared to the twigs and rougher bits in surface compost.

Variable results

The table of harvests shows much variation between vegetables, partly because of their season and partly because of their family. Digging damages mycorrhizal fungi in the soil, which work with the roots of many plants to help them source nutrients. Plants of the beet and brassica families, such as beetroot, cabbage, chard and turnips, do not use mycorrhizal association to improve their rooting, so are less disadvantaged by soil cultivation.

Left to right: potatoes, carrots, lettuce, spinach, parsnip. Slugs ate many carrot seedlings in the dug bed behind.

Parsnips are a little stronger in the undug bed on the left.

How no-dig works

Air is a vital ingredient of soil, but think of the soil underneath a lawn or a field of grazing animals, where the grass grows in spite of being walked and trodden on. This is because of an enduring structure of air channels in the soil, held in place by aggregations of organic matter and plant roots.

Soil for vegetable growing can be the same, but it does not have the roots of perennially present plants. We need to replace the structure these afford by adding organic matter to feed all the bacteria, fungi, nematodes and worms, helping *them* to maintain an open soil. They create soil structure far better than we can with tools and machinery.

Firm soil and compacted soil are not the same thing

Soil in a normal, firm, open state is often wrongly labelled as 'compacted soil'.

Put another way, *open is not the same as fluffy*. Soil that has been mechanically loosened and fluffed up is not in a stable state; hence the need to walk on planks after digging heavy soil, to avoid compaction. By contrast, it is actually difficult to compact a healthy, undug soil. I notice no damage from passing on wet clay with 200kg of wheelbarrow and manure. The wheel makes a visible impression but causes no permanent ruts and rain continues to soak in.

To illustrate this point when teaching a course I stand on some of my beds: I don't sink in or cause problems for the growing plants. And while walking around the garden on my permanent paths of soil, participants often comment on their springy feel – see the advice on paths in chapter 9.

True soil compaction

Compaction is caused by a combination of heavy pressure, moisture, soil disturbance and a lack of both organic matter and growing roots: for example, in over-cultivated fields and gardens during wet weather, especially just after cultivation, and on fields or building sites where big machines are passing on wet soil.

Compacted clay, orange and grey from lack of air.

Dense but open undug clay soil, with many plant roots, air channels and a worm.

Compacted soil is squishy when wet, rock-like when dry and more dead than alive. It contains few or no worm channels, is difficult to crumble in your hand and may smell sulphurous because of a lack of oxygen. Man-made compaction occurs mostly near the surface, in the top 15–20cm (6–8in), which should be possible to check with a spade. Compacted clay discolours, turning a dull grey or orange. If you see any of these signs, you need to add plenty of organic matter to the soil and then to be patient while it enables life to return.

When I took over the top field plot of soggy, compacted clay in 1999 I was unsure how to proceed, and took the simplest course of adding an inch or so of horse manure on the surface of 1.2m (4ft) wide strips, after shovelling some soil on to these beds from the 45cm (18in) pathways in between. I needed dry weather for spreading organic matter by wheelbarrow, because the soil was extremely sticky when wet.

The first year's harvests were embarrassing. As well as needing to hoe many annual weeds, I frequently used a trowel around the edges to remove roots of invading couch grass, whose spear-like roots are, in my experience, partly a response to soil compaction. I find they invade less now that the plot has more open soil.

In the autumn of 2000, when again spreading manure on all beds, I noticed the soil sticking less to my boots. This led to a more productive year in 2001, and the trajectory has been upwards ever since, with 2002 being a year when, at last, I felt proud of this plot.

Would progress have been quicker if I had dug and incorporated some organic matter?

Subsoil from 45cm (18in) below the surface of one of my undug beds, dense but crumbly.

I am not sure, but being patient did allow a stable soil structure to develop. The eventual outcome is superb, and shows the resilience of soil organisms, their ability to remedy a bad situation and that healing takes time.

'Soil pests'

A point that is often used to justify digging is: 'Soil pests are exposed and birds can eat them, or the gardener destroy them.' Maybe so, but *what about damage to all the good parts of soil life*? Do gardeners really want to expose their worms and have them eaten by birds?

I sometimes feel there is a belief that almost anything moving and living in soil, apart from earthworms, is a pest. I hope the evidence of this course helps you to appreciate the wonderful work done by soil's billions of inhabitants.

What is 'fertility'?

Soil fertility is often presented as a sufficiency of nutrients, meaning that there is enough food for plants. In fact this is just one part of the story. The other part of fertility is soil life: the presence of enough organisms both to make nutrients available, as when soil inhabitants die and are recycled into food, and to help plant roots feed on these nutrients.

Mycorrhizal fungi are a good example of biological fertility. In co-operation with many plants, their almost invisible filaments are able to travel long distances in search of nutrients needed by plants, which roots can then use. In return, the fungi are fed by carbohydrates travelling back down the roots, a product of photosynthesis by plants' leaves. So plants are fed and the fungi are fed, in an arrangement of mutual help called symbiosis.

If soil is cultivated, these beneficial fungi mostly die from being physically broken up and from being exposed to air and drying winds. Their need to recover, which my experiment suggests takes six to eight months, is a factor in some plants on dug soil being slower growing than those on undug beds, and sometimes then catching up later in the season.

Fungi in healthy soil producing mushrooms just after a December snowfall.

Life in the soil

In healthy soil there are huge numbers of a vast range of inhabitants, of all sizes, from microscopic bacteria and fungi to beetles and toads. They all have roles, and their roles all overlap and depend on others.

I suggest that leaving them all in peace is the kindest approach and most beneficial to us, since our plants can then grow better as a result of their undisturbed labours. Only a few soil organisms such as slugs, some pathogenic fungi and one or two nematodes are capable of harming our plants, and they do this mostly when we have made a wrong move, as in sowing tender seeds out of season: slugs then tidy up the seedlings, which they know are too weak to survive. In such situations, slugs are *doing their job*, which is to recycle garden waste, rather than being on a mission to destroy our plants. This is an example of how pests and diseases are usually teaching us a valuable lesson (see chapter 13).

Feed the soil rather than specific plants

Gardening becomes simple when the main emphasis is on looking after soil. Fertile soil can cater for the needs of a vast range of healthy plants, in all seasons, without the gardener needing to worry about the various requirements of each one.

For example, I often read advice to make a deep trench of organic matter before planting climbing beans. In fact you can avoid this huge amount of work and simply plant beans into surface-composted soil. Then it is sometimes advised that peas and beans do not actually need *any* compost or manure because they fix their own nitrogen, as do all legumes. But statements like this are a legacy of seeing fertility as a bundle of main nutrients needed by different plants, rather than as a store of life and vitality in the soil. Harvests are abundant when soil is well fed and well looked after.

Managing organic matter on the surface

Lastly a word on the slightly different methods of breaking up surface lumps of organic matter in a no-dig approach, as opposed to breaking up lumps of dug soil on top when organic matter has been incorporated.

Ideally the year's compost or manure is spread before Christmas, allowing time for frost, rain and drying winds to conduct a crumbling process. You can speed things up with a manure fork or rake – anything with prongs to knock the lumps of compost and encourage them to shatter. Short stints

of doing this during any dry spells in late winter should bring the surface to a soft, medium tilth, fine enough for most sowings and all plantings.

When lumps are large, I use a fork to hit them from above: the prongs' impact causes them to break apart. After another month or so, I use a rake to break the medium-sized lumps into smaller ones, moving it lightly through the surface compost and not in the soil below. Swinging a rake sideways is an effective way of creating a better tilth.

Compost and manure that is spread in spring and summer will often dry into lumps on top which, after some rain, can be broken up by walking over the surface of a bed, except when soil is saturated with water. The tilth is less fine than when compost is spread in winter.

Do remove any weeds you see when preparing ground at any time, even in winter. Clean soil harbours fewer slugs, and is always ready for sowing and planting.

Mature compost, eight months old. I turned the heap once.

CREATING A GROWING SPACE
CHOOSING A PLOT AND CLEANING THE SOIL

Vegetables need the sunniest position available, as far as possible from walls and trees. Start with a small area and crop it well; just one well-managed bed can be more productive than a larger, weedy plot. If as a beginner you are offered an allotment, a large space often full of weeds, look for a friend or two to share it with.

When starting with a new plot, be prepared to spend extra time clearing and composting weedy ground during the first year, to create clean and fertile soil. The first year is often the most challenging, but this initial expense of time and effort *will be repaid many times over* in years to come, when you will be sowing and reaping with only light weeding, instead of battling continually with weeds.

A suitable site

A perfect site for vegetable growing would enjoy full sunlight and some shelter from wind, with free-draining soil which also possessed enough body and organic matter to retain moisture in dry spells. Around the edge of this plot might be a clear area of mown grass or hard standing. Any trees or hedges would not be large enough to shade the growing area, or to suck moisture from it. Ground can be sloping but not so steeply that it is impossible to push a wheelbarrow.

Shade
Trees and hedges can be a difficult issue because their presence is so welcome, except for long shadows and their demands on nearby soil. A membrane placed on the soil,

at the bottom of a raised bed, offers some respite from foraging tree roots underneath. Small, thin gardens, with more edge than middle, offer difficult conditions for vegetables and need more skill in growing.

Extremely shady gardens are difficult for sun-loving, summer vegetables such as sweetcorn, courgettes and tomatoes, but

Soil is best kept clear before planting. Here there was surface debris harbouring slugs.

This plot was barren ten years ago with compacted soil, remedied simply by putting organic matter on top.

salads can work, slugs permitting. Slugs are a serious problem in damp shade and are often numerous in walls; for advice, see chapter 13.

Most enclosed areas receive some sun during summer and tomatoes may be possible, especially if there is a warm wall to hold the heat and give shelter. Container growing is worth considering, bearing in mind that container-grown vegetables need extra watering and are vulnerable to slugs. Where space is limited, salad plants offer the highest yield of tasty produce.

If shade is mostly from deciduous trees and shrubs, vegetables that do some of their growing in winter months are worth trying. Oriental salad leaves, land cress, corn salad, purple sprouting broccoli, kale, spring cabbage, garlic and overwintered broad beans should be possible.

Difficult soils

Hard, dense and stony soils can be significantly mitigated, and eventually improved, by constructing raised beds filled with fertile compost. Concentrating your time and resources on a small area is best, in the first year at least: start with just one or two beds of fertile ingredients, in the most favoured part of your site.

Allotments

If you have too little suitable space at home, taking on ground at an allotment is a next step. Before committing to it, reflect on how many spare hours you can give to a project that also involves time walking or driving to reach it.

My two main pieces of advice are to consider sharing an allotment, and to look closely at what you are offered before accepting.

Sharing offers mutual support and reduces the size of a plot to a more manageable level. Allotments were created for large families, growing serious amounts of food. Vegetables were relatively expensive, so there were stronger financial incentives to grow them than there are now, and people spent more time outdoors, with fewer alternative recreations.

If you have time and want to be self-sufficient in potatoes, cauliflower and onions, then a whole allotment is worth attempting. If your time is limited and you want mainly salads, green beans and courgettes, a quarter of an allotment is probably enough to take on.

Another reason for sharing is that, before handover to new holders, many allotment plots have suffered neglect, which allows large numbers of weeds to grow that are difficult to keep on top of and need to be patiently cleared before you start growing (see page 51).

Edges not hedges

Some interesting food-bearing plants can be grown on peripheral edges, such as carefully trained fruit trees, perhaps shaped as cordons or espaliers. These look attractive, produce lots of fruit and are not as difficult to achieve as you may imagine.

A major advantage of certain fruit trees over amenity hedging is that when grown on dwarfing rootstocks, such as M9 and M27 in the case of apples, they compete less with vegetables for moisture and nutrients.

Clearing ground

The advice here is for clearing derelict and neglected plots, as well as being applicable to existing gardens where hard-to-eradicate perennial weeds such as couch grass, ground elder and bindweed are continually taking valuable time to deal with.

For clearing large numbers of perennial weeds, my main advice is to use a long-term mulch. The methods you choose will depend on the time available, materials to hand and the weeds that are growing. For help in identifying your weeds – a first step in removing them is to establish the presence or not of perennial weeds – see chapter 6.

Perennial and annual weeds – a big difference

Perennial weeds such as couch grass and dandelion survive for aeons, thanks to food they store in long-lived roots, which often reach deep into the soil. They are the most difficult weeds to clear because of the time needed either to starve their roots with a mulch (a year or more) or to remove them by careful digging, and because many (not all) perennial weeds regrow from any small fragments of roots that are left behind when they are dug out.

Annual weeds such as meadow grass and sow (milk) thistle grow as new plants every year from seeds that lie in soil for a long time, often decades and more. Exposure of weeds to light allows germination, but seedlings are easy to remove when small in size and in number. They do not regrow from small fragments of roots and annual weeds can also be killed in four to six weeks by mulching.

Clearing perennial weeds

Easier examples When there are only a few perennial weeds, of kinds that do not regrow from small pieces of root – such as stinging nettle and dock, which because of their size

A neglected allotment. Weeds setting seed means hard work ahead.

BINDWEED – A SPECIAL CASE

Bindweed needs a special mention because of the 3–5m (10–16ft) depth to which its roots penetrate, making it impossible to dig out. Furthermore, some of its roots hold enough food to last for more than a year. Use a black polythene mulch for a whole year to deprive it completely of light. During this time any regrowth at the mulch edges must be regularly pulled, to stop it feeding the covered roots. Thereafter the bindweed is much weaker and any small green shoots that appear need removing when they are small, so that they do not have time to photosynthesize and send more food to the deep root system. Either pull them or use a trowel to extricate some root as well.

often look worse than they are – I suggest digging them out. Removing the top 10–15cm (4–6in) of a dock root and the central root cluster of a nettle clump is enough to prevent regrowth.

Woody plants such as brambles and thorn bushes should also be removed individually, because they can push new stems through any mulch. They are not too difficult to deal with, having relatively few root clusters: use a sharp spade to cut through their main stems just below surface level, and the remaining small roots do not regrow.

Most other perennials are more difficult to clear by digging out, especially bindweed and couch grass. The latter may also be hard to recognize among other grasses (see page 66), and is often present, especially in soils that have been over-cultivated and squashed.

Large amounts of these weeds justify extra time – probably a full year of mulching before you sow or plant any vegetables – and taking trouble to cover them most carefully. Time lost at the beginning, as you wait for weeds to wither in the absence of light, is then recovered many times over, as years of gardening on clean soil will free up your time.

Suitable mulches for suppressing perennial weeds

Cardboard is a freely available waste product that slowly decomposes *in situ* and adds to soil life. A second layer needs adding after two or three months. Large pieces of thick cardboard are the most useful and their edges need to overlap by 15cm (6in). Take care to remove tape and staples first and avoid cardboard that is laminated with thin layers of plastic.

Black plastic is effective as long as it is not torn or cut, in which case you can slide cardboard or more plastic under any holes. Unless it is of the more expensive woven kind, polythene does not allow water through and is best put on when ground is damp. Plastic sheets are good for windy sites and need to stay on for a whole growing season if the soil is choked with perennial weeds, to massively weaken all the roots. Most plastic mulches can be re-used often.

Layers of straw and lawn mowings can be used, but in time these become permeable to light and allow the more persistent weeds to regrow. They may also introduce some new weed seeds. Newspaper is difficult to use

ABOVE LEFT Cardboard overlapped and then covered with a little compost. You can also put compost below cardboard and weights on top. ABOVE Dandelion leaves much weakened but still growing, after six months' mulching. LEFT Porous black polythene suppresses most weed growth.

because of its smaller pieces, which take time to lay, and it blows around more easily than other mulches, but can be kept in place with 2.5cm (1cm) of compost on top.

Carpet is mostly unsuitable. Pieces of wool carpet are excellent for mulching weeds and leave no residue, but these are rare: nearly all carpets are now full of synthetic fibres, which end up disintegrating into horrible fragments, as sunlight gradually degrades them. They also contain chemical additives and are best avoided.

Keeping a mulch in place

Sheet mulches can be weighted down with stones or stakes, or in the case of cardboard lumps of compost and manure at corners and along edges. Cardboard rots more quickly under weights, so don't use too many. It can be covered with compost but it is then less effective as a mulch because it degrades faster; I prefer to put compost and manure down *before* laying cardboard on top. This way the soil is enriched as well as cleared: worms love to be busy under dark mulches.

When to apply mulches for suppressing perennial weeds

Weed-suppressing mulches are applied most effectively in late winter, just before new growth begins. This may be as early as January for grasses, as late as March for bindweed. Mulches can still be laid at any time, for instance in late summer as preparation for the following season's cropping.

Mulches that decompose, such as cardboard and straw, usually need another layer applied after two or three months, depending on how thick they were and on what weeds they were covering. Weeds such as couch grass will always need at least two applications of organic mulch, or a six-to-nine month covering with black polythene.

After mulching

Peek under your mulch after the time suggested to check that weeds have died. When a cover is removed, or has rotted away, the soil beneath should be clear of green leaves. A few perennial weeds may be weakly present, with some of their pale white roots visible near the surface, drawn upwards in search of light. You can ease these out with a trowel, pulling at the same time as levering the trowel to remove most of what is present in the top 10–15cm (4–6in) or so of soil.

Then you can shape or create some beds (see chapter 9) and plant them up. However, do persist with removing any regrowth of perennial weeds over the ensuing months, because if you leave just a few stems of couch grass or bindweed to enlarge and lengthen, they will soon recolonize a large area. I have seen this happen all too often, from a stage where the gardener was almost enjoying

clean soil. You are in a good position at the post-mulch stage, in sight of a really clean soil for easy vegetable growing: persevere and make the most of it!

Digging and rotovating to clear ground

If you do not mind digging, and have time to do it carefully, it is a way to remove most woody stems and perennial weeds, without having to wait for the roots to be starved by mulch. However, some roots of perennial weeds usually survive, especially couch grass and bindweed, so another forking through will be necessary after as little as two weeks in summer. Also many more annual weed seeds will germinate than when soil is cleared by mulching.

Rotovating perennial weeds has little to recommend it because the rotovator chops roots into pieces that simply grow again, *unless* there is a lengthy spell of warm, dry weather. You would have to rotovate at least three times, in dry and warm conditions throughout, to achieve a significant reduction in the population of perennial weeds.

Whether or not to use weedkillers

In a few situations I have used glyphosate – a systemic weedkiller which enters the sap of plants and weakens or kills them – painting it with a brush on leaves, preferably in summer when growth is vigorous. Only small amounts are needed but it is a poison, best kept for use as a last resort when the other methods described here are inappropriate: for instance, when bindweed is growing among plants you want to keep, so that a general mulch is not possible.

THICK MULCHES AND SLUGS

Many of these mulches offer shelter to slugs, which will probably eat seedlings of any carrots and lettuce sown immediately after you remove the mulch. At this stage it is better to grow faster and more slug-resistant vegetables: if it is springtime, plant onions or early potatoes, and in early summer, plant courgettes and leeks as a first vegetable. Slug numbers will gradually lessen after the mulching process, and also as you continue to keep soil clear of weeds.

CLEARING AN AREA OF WEEDS

1 May: grass and perennial weeds were first mulched in January with cardboard. Now potatoes are appearing through a second mulch of cardboard and straw, a roll of paper mulch at the back.

2 July: leeks behind the potatoes where the soil was mulched, red cabbage planted after potatoes were harvested in the front.

3 October: the last potatoes were followed by an August sowing of leaf radish; very few weeds.

4 August following: courgettes growing on soil that is now clear of any weeds.

AN ABSENCE OF WEEDS
VITAL KNOWLEDGE FOR AN ENJOYABLE PLOT

Here is a final piece of the weedy jigsaw. I explained in the previous chapter how to clear ground of all kinds of weeds, so what else could there be to say on the matter? Is it not now mainly a question of sowing seeds and waiting for harvests? No: I urge you to check this out first.

Why do weeds grow?

Germination of weed seeds is triggered by exposure of the seeds to light. Some farmers cultivate by night to avoid this happening. Dormant seeds also germinate in response to changes in temperature and moisture. This results in different weeds through the growing season, with never a dull moment!

Weeds are soil's way of keeping itself covered, of recycling nutrients, of increasing organic matter and also, I have come to suspect, of recovering an equilibrium that is disturbed by cultivation.

Fewer weeds germinate on undug soil because there is no need for it to re-cover, in the sense of recovering from cultivation. And the cover of a compost mulch seems to replicate, in part at least, the cover of growing plants. Surface-composted undug soil therefore grows fewer weeds than dug soil with compost incorporated.

However, some weed seeds blow in, and others arrive with dressings of compost and manure. I usually find a flush of new weed seedlings in spring, but they are easy to hoe or pull out of the friable compost, when still small.

Bindweed roots go down several feet but can be weakened by continually removing the top few inches of root.

A key understanding

Weeds are plants that we do not want because they mostly take light, water and food from our vegetables. This is the most common reason for removing them, but there is *another equally important and often overlooked reason* to keep on top of weeds. Weeds are extremely fast and efficient at reproducing themselves, either by root or by seed, and this leads to difficulties with the *next* sowings and plantings.

A gardener's weedy tale

So, for example, your onions have grown well and are bulbing up in early July. At this stage, their growth is not hampered by the weeds growing around them, and one could say that it is actually better for the soil to be covered (see 'Green manures' on page 17). It may also be the case that some other plants growing near the onions help them to ripen by depriving them of too many nutrients, especially nitrogen. However, allowing weeds to grow is extremely risky. If you leave the onions unweeded during their last few weeks, the tale can easily unfold along the following lines.

By the time you pull the onions in August, some weeds that have been allowed to grow will have set seed; others will have developed strong roots, so that they can't simply be pulled out, let alone hoed off, especially in a wet summer. Then it becomes a major task to grow more vegetables in that space, such as sowings of turnip and endive or a planting of bulb fennel, unless you spend a lot of time clearing the soil.

A different, cleaner story: stay involved

Instead of the above, what if you pull the small weed seedlings emerging among the onions as they mature in July? This takes much less time in the end, because small plants pull out so much more easily than large ones. Two quick weedings in July will keep the ground clean, and you can quickly pull any weed seedlings in early August when you harvest the onions.

Then, in the clean soil, it is simple to draw a drill for seeds of turnip, endive, rocket and oriental salad leaves, or to dib holes

A mass of fat hen seedlings in May – the result of plants dropping seeds the previous autumn.

for plants of late calabrese, bulb fennel and radicchio, and subsequently to continue with occasional small amounts of weeding until season's end. By that time you will have enjoyed a second harvest; the soil will still be clean, ready for some compost, and you can look forward to next year without dread of new sowings being engulfed by weeds.

Little and often

The theme of these tales is to do frequent, quick weeding, in just a small way, as often as you can. Sorry if this sounds unglamorous and less appealing than planting and picking, but maintaining a productive plot, without undue effort, is really about clever, continual, speedy maintenance, of which a key part is being on top of weed growth at all times. It actually becomes enjoyable when the number of weeds diminishes.

Is this too disciplinarian? Should one not relax more, let nature do its thing and see where it leads? I have seen the results of that approach far too often and know the consequence all too well: a weedy mess where sowing is almost impossible and most of the gardener's time is needed for sorting out the chaos of unwanted plants. Also, in damp climates, there are problems with the slugs that weeds give shelter to.

I have seen gardeners spending huge amounts of time and money on clearing gardens and allotments, achieving a lovely clean soil, and then demonstrating a seeming aversion to pulling a few, *only a few*, weeds, which then drop thousands of seeds. They could have avoided the resulting explosion of weed seedlings so easily by taking just a few minutes to pull their parents.

THE MAIN PRINCIPLES OF LITTLE-AND-OFTEN WEEDING

- Keep your eyes open and train them to notice weed seedlings at all times. Weeds grow fast and have an uncanny ability to be invisible, until suddenly they have flowered and are shedding lots of seeds.
- Be happy to pull the weeds you notice unexpectedly, even when doing something else, because you know that it is a vital part of creating an easy-to-run garden or allotment.
- Soil that is permanently clean opens many possibilities for new sowings at any stage, leading to a virtuous circle of soil that is kept clean for a reason, and vegetables that need only light weeding, through all the season.
- Having a continual series of sowings and plantings means that there is more to eat!

How much weeding?

Once your initial clearances and mulching have cleaned the soil of perennial weed roots, most subsequent weeding will be of small, newly germinated weed seedlings. How many weed seeds germinate will depend on whether you dug or mulched to remove any perennials.

After digging there will be a relative explosion of weed seedlings and hoeing is the quickest way to deal with them: see below.

After mulching to remove perennial weeds, and especially in soil which has a thin covering of mostly weed-free compost and manure on top, few new weeds will grow and much less weeding will be needed: just a small weeding every fortnight or so.

I recommend you also go looking for new weeds under the leaves of spreading vegetables such as calabrese and squashes, to avoid any growing enough to flower and seed while out of sight.

More mulching?

Once soil is clean, it is possible to continue preventing weeds growing with a permanent plastic mulch, *but it is also entirely possible to manage without a permanent mulch.* Sheets of plastic encourage slugs and look much less attractive than dark, composted soil. Cardboard is invaluable for cleaning soil initially but less suitable when growing closely spaced vegetables.

Hoeing

Hoeing is a valuable skill to develop for the cropping of large plots. Best results come from hoeing when weed roots are young, thin and fragile. The soil needs to be reasonably dry, or the sun bright. Hoe when weeds are small, because large ones are less inclined to die when hoed, as are many grasses whose roots are amazingly enduring

Aim to *move as little soil as possible*: just enough to disturb or cut through weed roots. If you hoe too deeply, you will simply move weeds, with soil on their roots, to a new location. Shallow hoeing takes less energy and can quickly clear large areas of

Weed seedlings at an ideal size for hoeing.

After hoeing the tiny weeds are unlikely to recover.

many hundreds or thousands of seedlings. Enjoy picturing, as you do this, the time it would have taken to deal with those weeds had you left them to grow.

Green manures

Growing green manures between harvests of vegetables is a way of keeping soil covered and maintaining fertility. Consequently there will be less need to import organic matter, as long as the ground is not required for growing food (a major caveat: see below).

Compared to spreading bought-in compost and manure, green manures are sometimes a cheaper, simpler and less resource-intensive way of slightly enriching soil. Sowings of clover, phacelia, buckwheat and grazing rye can be effective in large plots, sown after growing one vegetable per season, and if digging is done as part of soil preparation, incorporating them will not be extra work.

However, in a small plot, where the aim is to enjoy harvests as much of the time as possible, often through second cropping,

there is not room for green manures. It is simpler and more productive to buy the relatively small amount of additional organic matter needed to maintain fertility, spread it in late autumn and grow vegetables continuously throughout the season. This is more effective than sowing a green manure that will need to be dug in, will remove nutrients from growing crops while it is decomposing and will offer habitat for slugs and opportunities for new weeds, because of both digging and weeds going to seed during the growth of the green manure.

Two exceptions are Persian clover (*Trifolium resupinatum*) and mustard (*Brassica juncea*), which both grow fast and are killed by frost of about −7°C/19°F or lower, so there is no need to smother or incorporate them. The former can be sown from July to August and the latter from August to early September, but *only if you are not wanting to sow any more vegetables at those times*. I recommend weeding these green manures in exactly the same way as if they were plants for eating.

Annual weeds: some common examples

This selection is to help you identify and deal with some likely and unwanted appearances in your plot. Ideally you will hoe them when they are too small for you to identify any flowering stems, and after a year of doing that, your soil will have far fewer weed seedlings.

When large, almost all weeds are better pulled and removed, but as seedlings they can be hoed. Since hoeing removes more weeds for less effort, this reinforces the point that weeds are best dealt with small.

Unlike perennial weeds, annuals do not regrow from small roots left in the soil, the main aim is to cut their stem just below the point where roots branch out in all directions, so that remaining roots become separated and therefore lack any ability to channel growth. By contrast, thick stands of annual weeds can be killed by mulches in four to six weeks.

▲ Bittercress, hairy (*Cardamine hirsuta*)

DESCRIPTION 2.5–5cm high (1–2in), tiny white flowers

SEEDING Sets seed in four to six weeks

Mostly a winter weed of cool, moist soil, small enough to go unnoticed until it scatters hundreds of long-lived seeds at a young age, so keep an eye out for it in spells of consistently damp and cool weather. The small leaves are edible and tasty.

◄ Charlock (*Brassica arvensis*)

DESCRIPTION Up to 60cm (24in) high, pale yellow flowers

SEEDING Sets seed in eight to ten weeks

Germinates all through the seasons, mostly in spring, and can also overwinter. A fast-growing weed of the brassica family, often full of flea beetle damage but still able to set hundreds of seeds. Easy to hoe when small and easy to pull when larger, but don't underestimate its ability to gain ground through numerical superiority.

▲ Chickweed (*Stellaria media*)

DESCRIPTION 5–7cm (2–3in) high, vigorous spreading habit, small white flowers, strong root system

SEEDING Can set seed within a month

Probably the most common annual weed, it germinates in damp soil, chiefly in early spring and autumn and in mild winters too. The odd plant here and there is easy to remove but its ability to set seed quickly can lead to problems, because it is often too damp for hoeing when chickweed grows. Watch for it at all times and hoe seedlings or pull any small plants you see, with a firm tug because they have tenacious, if shallow roots.

▲ Fat hen (*Chenopodium album*)

DESCRIPTION Up to 75cm (30in) high, nondescript green flowers

SEEDING Forms clusters of many pale green seeds within six weeks, mostly in summer

A weed of rich soil (shown above around a broad bean plant), related to orach and tree spinach with spinach-like leaves, edible raw when small or cooked when larger. Seedlings germinate readily and often in great number; they are tiny at first and look quite innocent, but subsequent growth belies this and plants grow large in moist, rich soil or on manure heaps. Hoeing when small is the simplest way to deal with large numbers, often twice; then hand weed any that survive.

◀ Grass, annual meadow (*Poa annua*)

DESCRIPTION 2.5–5cm (1–2in) high, tiny feathery flowers

SEEDING Sets seed in six to eight weeks in any season

A small, tough and common plant, growing whenever it is mild and moist for a couple of weeks. Roots are numerous but superficial, survive waterlogging but dislike drought. Common in mild winters and in any other

damp season, it is difficult to hoe and best pulled when small. Larger clumps have tenacious roots which hang on to a lot of soil – a bad loss to the garden and a bad addition to the compost heap, where any larger amounts of soil can slow heating and decomposition of the other ingredients.

▶ Groundsel (*Senecio vulgaris*)

DESCRIPTION 5–22cm (2–9in) high, clustered small yellow flowers

SEEDING Sets seed within four to six weeks An easy weed to hoe but not to be underestimated, because even one plant, setting hundreds of seeds after only a few weeks' growth, can lead to much extra weeding in subsequent years. Germinates at all times except midwinter, mostly in fertile soil; sets seed when small and young if soil is dry or shady. Check for odd plants under leaves of, for instance, parsnips, courgettes and asparagus. Go hunt them! Remove any with flowers, as they can still make viable seed if uprooted but left on the soil.

▼ Oxalis

DESCRIPTION Only 5cm (2in) high but has an ability to seed prolifically

SEEDING Drops seed from scarcely visible pods, often before you notice its presence Often arrives with pot plants. Needs vigilance once present because it multiplies fast. There are red- and green-leaved types.

▼ Shepherd's purse (*Capsella bursa-pastoris*)

DESCRIPTION 5–10cm (2–4in) high, cluster of pointed leaves and a tall, spiky flowering stem

SEEDING Sets seed in six to eight weeks Most easily recognized by its stem of green seed pods (purses). Do remove plants before any can drop seeds, for by that time there is a vigorous tap root which may be hard to pull out, although plants can be killed by cutting the main root with a hoe or trowel.

▲ Sow (milk) thistle, prickly (*Sonchus asper*)

DESCRIPTION Up to 90cm (36in) high but often smaller, pale yellow flowers

SEEDING Sets seed in as little as four weeks when in dry or shaded conditions

Another weed that needs vigilance, with a strong tap root and rapid development of hundreds of seeds. Germinates in a wide variety of conditions; is most common in late summer and autumn; may even overwinter; leaves are less prickly than those of creeping thistle. There is also a perennial sow thistle (*Sonchus arvensis*), whose fleshy roots are quick to colonize, but plants can be removed as seedlings to prevent them from invading.

▲ Speedwell, common field (*Veronica persica*)

DESCRIPTION Ground-hugging spring and autumn weed, slender stems, pale blue flowers

SEEDING Sets seed in four to six weeks

Of the many kinds of speedwell, including perennial ones, this common annual is the most likely to grow, in early spring and late autumn, and is not too difficult to hoe or pull out when small, mostly from March to May, but becomes difficult if allowed to establish as larger clumps of many plants. Slender speedwell looks similar but does not set seed and spreads by root fragments.

Squash plants were covered with fleece for eighteen days in May but only a few small weeds grew and I am pulling them all.

Perennial weeds: some common examples

The times given for each weed here are an indication of how long they need covering with a mulch that excludes all light, so that food reserves in their roots are exhausted by continual attempts at regrowing in darkness.

Reducing the time of covering will result in some regrowth that you must keep on top of, or else you may soon be back to the weedy mess you began with. Patience is a vital part of all effective mulching to eradicate persistent weeds.

A mulch is most effective when laid in early spring, so that new growth from established roots is continually frustrated by the lack of light, until the roots become exhausted and wither.

Here is a list of some common ones, with ideas of what it takes to clear them completely.

▼ Bindweed
TIME/EASE OF CLEARING One year minimum; some regrowth occurs
Hedge bindweed or bellbind (*Calystegia sepium*) is a vigorous climber with white,

trumpet-like flowers and thick, fleshy roots, many of which lie close to the surface. Field bindweed (*Convolvulus arvensis*) has smaller leaves, thinner roots and white or pink flowers that are more discrete.

I have found it possible to eradicate minor infestations of hedge bindweed by persisting for a year, with a combination of using a trowel to lever out any accessible roots, and pulling all its small stems as soon as I see them, to starve roots that cannot be reached, as often happens when bindweed is growing among other plants.

Field bindweed is less visible but more enduring, and even when frequently pulled or dug out, it often spreads in from an edge. An initial mulch is helpful in reducing its vigour, after which I find that infested areas become manageable with frequent but small amounts of trowel work.

▼ Bramble (*Rubus fruticosus*)
TIME/EASE OF CLEARING Best removed manually; cut and burn stems first
Brambles look worse than they are and careful digging out of the main root stems should see them gone: smaller secondary roots can be left in the soil. Mulching is

less effective, as the strong stems can push up through it. New seedlings need pulling out when small and invading stems need trimming.

▲ Buttercup, creeping (*Ranunculus repens*)

TIME/EASE OF CLEARING Six months, preferably from late winter to early summer

Large amounts of buttercup are hard to remove by digging out because the roots are tenacious, although quite shallow. Mulching is effective within six to eight months (less in the growing season); subsequent buttercups will grow only from seed and can be hoed. Also in this family is *celandine* (*Ranunculus ficaria*), whose tuberous roots are tricky to extricate, and although its flowers are pretty, I recommend removal from the vegetable plot whenever you notice them, or mulching any thick infestation.

▲ Couch grass, quack grass, twitch (*Agropyron repens*)

TIME/EASE OF CLEARING One year, vigorous regrowth from root fragments and invasive from weedy edges

This weed with spear-like, creeping rhizomes is all too common, often in soil that has been either compacted or over-cultivated at some stage. Hence it responds well, if slowly, to soil enrichment without cultivation and with surface mulching. I have cleared some thick infestations within a year, but two years is more realistic to be completely clear, and even then new roots can spread in from uncleared edges. I use a sharp trowel to remove these new spears, every four to six weeks in summer, before they become too established.

So if couch is established everywhere, as on some allotments I have seen, a whole year of light-excluding mulch can be followed by planting a few widely spaced vegetables in the second year, such as courgettes or squashes, while you still pull any couch regrowth.

▲ Creeping thistle (*Cirsium arvense*)

TIME/EASE OF CLEARING Twelve months; can be eradicated by persistent pulling of small plants

A glove is invaluable in dealing with odd plants of this prickly thistle. Insert your gloved fingers below the leaves and gently grasp its fleshy but firm stem; then pull smoothly, aiming to remove 7–10cm (3–4in) of white root that has grown up from much deeper roots. I once cleared a large, dense patch of such thistles by repeatedly pulling them in this way, over about eighteen months. Keep pulling, even when there are only one or two, to totally exhaust the parent roots. Persistence pays off and this weed, although initially daunting, can be completely eradicated, manually or by mulch. Beware also of creeping sow thistle (page 64), which can also be invasive if not pulled when small.

▲ Dandelion (*Taraxacum officinale*)

TIME/EASE OF CLEARING Six to nine months; remove any weakened survivors with a trowel

Small numbers can be dug out with a spade: aim to remove 15cm (6in) or more of older roots, so that there is too little left in the soil for viable regrowth. Mulching dandelions works well but takes the best part of a growing season, and is most effective when starting before the end of winter, as soon as leaves are growing again.

Although a common weed, persisting both from root fragments and rapid germination of its many seeds, dandelion has many medicinal and culinary uses. Along with common salads such as lettuce and endive, dandelion is a member of the *Asteraceae* family. Its generic name derives from *taraxos*, meaning disorder, and *akos*, remedy. The leaves are diuretic, cleansing for the liver and rich in minerals, and can be eaten in salads. Roots dug out in autumn can be dried, roasted at 200°C/392°F and then ground to make a dark, earthy drink that is wrongly called a coffee substitute; I would call it an acquired taste!

▲ Dock, broad-leaved (*Rumex obtusifolius*) and curled (*R. crispus*)

TIME/EASE OF CLEARING One year – but it is often easier to dig out with a sharp spade

Docks of both types are less onerous than they look, but do not allow them to set seed. The large, dark, ugly leaves have an imposing presence but a sharp spade can be sliced through taproots about 15cm (6in) down; the remaining root does not normally regrow. Smaller docks can be pulled if soil is soft and moist; otherwise use a trowel. When the seed heads are mature with clusters of brown seeds, I recommend burning them; dock plants without seed can be composted when mixed with enough other leaves to raise the temperature.

Dock leaves have a use: to rub on skin which has been stung by nettles. They host a beetle that also, unfortunately, eats sorrel leaves.

▲ Ground elder (*Aegopodium podagraria*)

TIME/EASE OF CLEARING One year; some weak regrowth, but this is eradicable

The roots are tough, medium thick, white and tend to snap as they are being pulled out; use a trowel or fork to follow them as far as possible. They travel horizontally more than vertically and entwine around roots of other plants, making removal difficult except in soil that has no other plants growing in it. In that case, thorough mulching, or digging and extraction of every root fragment, will be effective.

Ground elder has culinary possibilities; it is a member of the umbellifer family and was introduced by the Romans for its edible leaves. Eat them raw or steamed, and as a filling in omelettes – they are not a delicacy but are available, and most tasty, in early spring when other vegetables are scarce.

▲ Mare's tail, horsetail, paddy's pipe (*Equisetum hyemale*)

TIME/EASE OF CLEARING One year
minimum; some regrowth occurs

An extremely vigorous and deep-rooting
weed, whose spiky stems and leaves appear
as remnants of a prehistoric time. Thankfully
less common than couch grass, but even
more persistent, especially in soil that
lies damp. A long mulch is a good start,
followed by persistent hoeing; I have heard
of gardeners eradicating it within three years,
and others struggling with it for a decade.

▶ Rosebay willowherb (*Chamerion angustifolium*)

TIME/EASE OF CLEARING Six months; or
remove manually

An invasive weed, both from seed and root.
Initial rosettes of shiny leaves can be mistaken
for lamb's lettuce; if left to grow, these
develop tenacious roots and then send out

white, fleshy stems below soil level, which
endure for many years but are not too difficult
to eradicate. Pretty pink flowers on a long
stem in late summer turn quickly to hundreds
of feathery seeds; if this occurs, rosebay
willlowherb can be a problem for many years.

▲ Stinging nettle, common nettle (*Urtica dioica*)

TIME/EASE OF CLEARING Six to nine
months; or remove manually

A sign of rich soil and not too difficult to
remove, but wear gloves when handling large
plants, using a fork to lever out the main
clump of pale yellow roots. Smaller roots do
not regrow. Seeding is prolific and seedlings
can be hoed.

ORGANIC MATTERS
QUALITY, EASE OF USE AND COST

Adding decomposed organic matter to soil brings enduring improvements to growth, so access to a reliable source is invaluable to gardeners. The most dependable and often most valuable compost you can use is from your own bin or heap. Making it can be done in many ways that are explained in chapter 8.

What else to look for? The answer has become both simpler and more complicated in recent years. Simpler because of the widespread composting of green waste by many local authorities and corporations. More complicated because of the insufficiently regulated presence of toxic chemicals in a few of these composts and manures.

Organic matter can also be used in a 'raw' state, as when mulching bushes and larger plants with freshly mown grass or cardboard, with benefits to soil and plants that are slower and of a different nature, but of less value to most vegetables.

Composts and manures

These words can mislead because they are used to describe such a wide range of material. For example, 'manure' is mostly now understood as coming from animals but the word is occasionally used for general compost, and even for synthetic fertilizers. So I will start by clarifying the language, before comparing different products.

Compost

Compost is the dark-coloured residue of decomposed plant materials and animal excretions. Variable ingredients, assembled in different ways and at different times of year, make composts of vastly different qualities. All have value, some more than others and in different situations.

Summer lettuce is often short of moisture but these plants are thriving in soil enriched with compost for many years.

GARDEN COMPOST A variable product! Any gardener with a little space for a heap or container, and some raw materials, should have a go at making some. For help with this, see chapter 8.

GREEN WASTE COMPOST from the fermentation of household and garden wastes. Powerful shredders are used to chop all ingredients, including woody ones, into small enough pieces for rapid heating to occur, so that few weed seeds and pathogens survive. The process is made faster by frequent turning of heaps. A large percentage of woody ingredients can temporarily rob soil of nutrients if the compost is dug in; see 'A trial' on page 74.

MUSHROOM COMPOST A 'waste product' after it has been used to grow crops of mushrooms in dark sheds or tunnels. The ingredients are mainly straw, with some horse or chicken manure, peat and plenty of fungal mycelium. There are fewer nutrients than in animal manures.

Green waste compost with bits of wood.

One-year-old mushroom compost for potting.

POTTING, MULTIPURPOSE COMPOST

is sold by the sack and the quality is uncertain. It was previously made with peat, and now often with green waste compost, mixed with nutrient-rich ingredients to make a concentrated growing medium for plants in trays, pots, containers and growing bags. It is usually called multipurpose compost and is expensive for spreading in the garden; if you do, be sure to use organic compost, whose nutrients will not leach away in winter or in heavy rain.

VERMICOMPOST Worm casts. The dark, soft residue of worm farming (or of worm-eaten garden compost or animal manure) is a rich and soft compost.

Manure

Manure is excrement from animals such as horses, cows, pigs, sheep and poultry, together with any bedding they have lain on. This is usually one or more of cereal straw, shredded paper, hemp and woodchips.

The value of manure depends on how long it has been composted in a heap, how much bedding was used and of which kind, and whether the heap has been looked after, for example with no weeds being allowed to seed on to it. There are great possibilities in any animal manure that has spent several months in a tidy heap.

Fresh manure, with its identifiable ingredients of animal faeces and

RESIDUE CHECK FOR ANIMAL MANURE

Before having any manure delivered, see if you can obtain a small bucketful, preferably well rotted. Put some in a seed tray, box or large pot, mixed with a little soil, and sow or plant salads, broad bean, pea or tomato – any or all. Keep in a warm place to speed up growth and within three or four weeks you should have some healthy growth, indicating the absence of harmful herbicides. But if leaves curl upwards, this suggests aminopyralid residues and you need to look elsewhere.

Horse manure with many weed seedlings.

How not to look after a heap of organic matter: spreading nettles and weeds.

undecomposed bedding such as yellow straw, should be composted in a heap for four to six months at least, or up to a year for best results, until it is generally dark brown and showing signs of becoming crumbly.

Chemical residues can cause problems, for instance if the animals' food has included grass or hay from pastures sprayed with herbicides containing aminopyralids. A farmer should be able to tell you if asked, but horse owners probably won't know how the hay was grown. Also, poultry and pig manure from intensive farming may be contaminated with antibiotics and other drugs.

Quality

Commercial green waste composts are of extremely variable quality, even when they look quite similar; in Britain, they must at least meet the PAS 100 guidelines, a certified industry standard. Usually the heaps have been hot enough to kill all weed residues and any pathogens, but the heat may also have been intense enough to 'cook' the compost, almost carbonizing it, leaving it with a possible lack of bacteria and fungi.

Mushroom compost may contain pesticide residues, although more mushroom farmers now use predators to control their pests and some grow organically. The compost has great value as a weed-free mulch and it enriches soil with lively organic matter. Should it be light brown and strawy when purchased or delivered, I suggest leaving it in a heap to decompose further for two or three months, unless it is for mulching bushes and borders.

Animal manures have more nutrients, but their quality and ease of use is variable, according to their age and the kind of animal and type of bedding used: straw, for example, helps the manure to rot more quickly than a bedding of wood shavings.

Worm compost is excellent for growing plants in pots or containers, or for improving all soils. Use it sparingly, because it is expensive to produce: a lot of worms are needed to make a small amount of compost, and home wormeries need careful and time-consuming management!

Labels may be misleading: for instance, I bought a sack of 'Organic Farmyard Manure'

Less-rotted manure.

More-rotted manure.

which, when opened, revealed itself as woody, green waste compost. Bags coming from a 'farm' with photos of animals may not contain animal manure!

Ease of use

Mushroom and green waste compost are mostly soft, fluffy and easy to spread, with few large lumps. Home-made compost and animal manures are often lumpier, but if spread in autumn (see page 79), allowing a whole winter's weather to break them up, with the aid of some light raking they can become fine and of good consistency for spring sowing and planting.

Lumpy compost can be spread as a mulch around vegetables that are already growing, such as courgettes, climbing beans and brassicas, and between rows of parsnips, celeriac, carrots, leeks and garlic. It will finish decomposing as they grow and improve the soil for a succeeding vegetable.

A trial

One July I potted some month-old lettuce plants into four pots of different composts and manure. The plants grew until

November and I harvested some outer leaves every three weeks from all except the lettuce in green waste compost. No liquid feed was used.

Garden compost that had been sieved and was a year old gave the strongest, longest-growing plant compared with those growing in old cow manure and multipurpose, organic potting compost: lettuce in the latter grew fast in the first month and then weakened. The green waste compost gave a weak, yellow plant at first but its colour (not size) improved after two months, when some of the wood had finished decomposing (see illustrations opposite).

Cost

Quality and ease of use vary so much that value for money is hard to assign. I suggest that £20 per tonne delivered is reasonable. Year-old animal manure is more valuable than green waste compost whose main ingredients are less rich in nutrients. One tonne is enough for spreading about 2–3cm (1in) of compost or manure on a 60–80m length of beds which are 1.2m wide (4 × 200–260 feet), or half to two-thirds of a 10-

11 August: four plants of lettuce 'Mottistone', planted on 26 July in different composts.

19 August: the same lettuce, in green waste and West Riding compost in the front (left to right), and manure and my own compost at the back.

Mid-September before the second pick. No feeds were given at any stage.

Mid-October: the green waste compost is finally releasing some nutrients but my own compost has the most at this stage.

rod allotment. There can be twelve to thirty wheelbarrow loads per tonne, depending on the size of your barrow.

A major part of the cost is transport, so if you can collect compost in your own trailer, unbagged, it will be much cheaper; many car trailers hold more than half a tonne. Or have several tons delivered and share it with neighbours. If someone offers to deliver a 'trailerload', check how heavy it will be to have an idea of quantity.

For a first season of thick mulching (7–10cm/3–4in), to improve soil and reduce weed growth, a 6-ton load would be needed to cover the beds of a 10-rod allotment. Thereafter one or two tonnes per annum is enough to keep improving the soil, which can be supplied with two or three home-made heaps if they are being filled from a larger garden, for instance with grass and leaves. You cannot make enough compost just from the residues of a vegetable plot.

Uncomposted organic matters

Organic matter which has not decomposed is mostly unsuitable for vegetable growing, except perhaps around larger, established plants. Raw mulches encourage slugs and make sowing difficult. Also they must never be incorporated because soil nutrients will be used in their decomposition, rather than for growing plants.

CARDBOARD AND PAPER One layer of thick cardboard can last long enough to kill the grass of a lawn or pasture; thinner cardboard decomposes after two or three months and then needs another layer on top. If there is couch grass or bindweed, a third layer may be needed later. There have been concerns about old ink in recycled cardboard but I still use it occasionally.

COMFREY Of all leaves to use as a mulch, or for making a liquid feed (see opposite), comfrey is probably the richest in plant food. Be sure to plant roots of Bocking comfrey, which does not flower and set seed (see page 200). Otherwise you will have plants all over the garden and the plant's deep taproot, sourcing minerals, makes it extremely hard to remove.

GRASS MOWINGS Best used in layers no more than 2.5–5cm (1–2in) thick; any thicker means they can pack down in wet weather and create an anaerobic layer, which is not healthy for the soil below. Similar care is needed when adding grass to compost heaps, but it has great value there in helping to create heat (see Chapter 8).

LEAVES are a rich food for soil, but for growing vegetables they need composting first, for at least a year, or even two years. When they are shredded and mixed with green matter and animal manure, an excellent compost is possible. Spreading leaves in their raw state is good for trees and shrubs.

SEAWEED Coastal residents are well placed for access to one of nature's most complete foods. The rest of us have to make do with occasional use of a proprietary sea product, such as seaweed meal or liquid feed. These are expensive but even in small doses the extensive range of minerals they provide can raise plants to a new level of health.

WOOD CHIPS AND SAWDUST Wood chips have uses in ornamental borders, but they last for two or three years and may be obstructive if, for example, you need to remove perennial weeds growing through them. Woody material should not be incorporated into soil, where its decomposition process takes nutrients from growing plants. Sawdust rots quite quickly on the surface and can be used as a mulch when growing vegetables.

Wood chips, mostly unrotted.

Other products

The organic matters listed here have specific uses and are mostly more expensive.

BLOOD, FISH AND BONEMEAL This may boost the growth of your plants but is a costly product to use; I would say it is unnecessary if you are spreading compost and manure, as recommended here.

CHICKEN MANURE PELLETS These are less organic matter and more a concentrated source of nutrients. Use sparingly, perhaps with green waste compost.

COMFREY Liquid feeds are chiefly for tomatoes and container-grown plants. You can make your own by squashing comfrey leaves into a bucket or barrel, with only a little water, until the liquid turns black and is often ready to use within a week. Dilute it before watering on to plants in pots and containers. Stinging nettle leaves and stems can also be processed in the same way as comfrey to make a rich plant food, but these feeds are extremely smelly and unpleasant to use.

ERICACEOUS COMPOST is acid (low pH), for growing plants such as blueberries and cranberries in enclosed beds or large pots.

ROCKDUST Crushed basalt (volcanic rock) has a balanced and wide range of useful minerals; sprinkle it on the surface at any time of year, up to 1cm (½in) thick if you can afford it. The value of rockdust is hard to quantify; it should give more value on poor soils. Look out for Lavadust, the extremely fine powder of volcanic lava which I have found more effective than rockdust.

Using organic matter

Simplicity

Simple methods work best. Organic matter on the surface is a copy of how things work in nature where man is not involved: decomposing organic matter lies on top of the soil, decays and then 'disappears', taken into the soil by different organisms.

The problem with transferring this model to vegetable growing is that gardens do not happen in nature. We are creating a somewhat unnatural environment, with more bare soil than usual. Even organic vegetables, in this sense, are 'unnatural'.

Permaculturists solve this problem by creating gardens without bare soil and full of perennial vegetables, bushes and trees. However, in such a garden it is difficult to grow annual vegetables such as carrots, parsnips and lettuce, so you still need a patch of clear ground for growing these. Also the range of perennial vegetables, although interesting, is neither extensive nor likely to feed you for long periods from small areas.

To grow annual vegetables continuously in the same ground, a weed-free surface is essential: initially, to have successful germination with fewer pests around, and later for growth to be abundant without the competition of weeds.

I suggest that treating bare, undug soil with surface mulches of compost is a way of replicating nature's principles, if not her methods, effectively using the composting process as a shortcut. This means there is organic matter on the surface which is suitable for sowing and planting vegetables into. The unnatural environment of soil that is bare for some of the year is compensated by compost providing food and undisturbed shelter for all its organisms. Once vegetables are growing, their leaves cover the soil and nature is assuaged. This is the easy time in vegetable growing. The more tricky part can be managing a plot when it is empty, and this is where compost plays a key role.

Enriching the surface all the time

In my garden I am often asked why the soil level is not rising, because of my annual spreading of 2.5–5cm (1–2in) compost on the beds. I suggest that without such additions the soil level would actually descend. I can see

this in a polytunnel where I add 5cm (2in) of compost and manure every spring, yet the level inside is no higher than the level of soil under the grass on the plastic's outer side, where the growing and decaying of grass and its roots is a similar continuous cycle of soil maintenance and improvement.

Organic matter on the surface benefits all kinds of wildlife. The soil food chain is strengthened with extra bacteria, fungi, grubs, worms and beetles among other soil inhabitants. These soil inhabitants provide regular food for more visible members of the above-ground food chain, such as birds, hedgehogs, slow worms, badgers and even slugs and snails. All play a role in helping to maintain a healthy, humming balance of life and of nutrients for growing plants.

Does organic matter need to be incorporated?

Digging compost and manure into the soil, as often recommended, is called

BELOW LEFT Salad plants in April in an unheated polytunnel. They have been regularly harvested since November.
CENTRE The salad plants are cleared as they flower and 2.5–5cm (1–2in) of well-rotted manure is spread on the soil surface.
FAR RIGHT Summer vegetables – cucumber, tomato, basil and aubergine – are planted into and through the surface manure.

WHEN TO SPREAD COMPOST

Any time of year is possible, for instance when using compost as a mulch around established plants. Less-rotted compost can be used to mulch larger vegetables in early summer, or spread after a final harvest in autumn, to finish breaking down in surface air.

If there is a clear choice, *spreading in autumn* gives best results: the soil is usually moist and warm enough then for organisms to busy themselves with feeding on the new goodies and to distribute them widely. Then the compost is broken down by winter weather, becoming soft and more friable by spring. See also 'Using compost', page 14.

incorporation. The supposed idea is that doing so places organic matter 'closer to plant roots'. But, as well as shattering the existing soil structure, this ignores the fact that most plants root extensively in the top few inches. For example, just below surface level, when the soil is moist, I find fibrous roots of courgette, salad, chard, chicory, spinach and so forth. Parsnips too! It is therefore baffling to me that so many gardeners eschew the benefits of spreading

organic matter on top. Similarly, when planting trees, fill the hole with soil only and then mulch with organic matter.

When soil life is undisturbed and allowed to 'get busy' dealing with organic matter on the surface, an undug area has plenty of nutrients at a greater depth, without them having to be put there by digging, because the soil inhabitants are continually moving them around and incorporating them more efficiently than we ever can.

YOUR OWN COMPOST
A KEY INGREDIENT IS PATIENCE

Transforming waste materials into compost is fun, even though the home-made version can be lumpy and fibrous rather than light and even. Despite this, it contains much goodness: home-made compost is often more full of life-enhancing bacteria and fungi than many over-heated commercial composts, and if you have room to leave it a year, from start to finish, there is a good chance of finding some lovely stuff in the older parts of your heap. It can be forked out and spread on soil at any time of year (see page 79). Fine, crumbly compost can be sieved for use in potting: see chapter 10.

This chapter is laid out as answers to the questions I am most frequently asked about composting. There are many ways to create it, bearing in mind these principles.

Why make compost?

Garden and kitchen produce unwanted weeds, trimmings and vegetable residues. These can be gathered together in a tidy heap to decompose, which turns them into a valuable food for soil and for plants, with living organisms and nutrients.

How difficult is it?

You will mostly succeed but you may not obtain the compost of your dreams on a regular basis. Making compost is fascinating, as every batch is different, because of the continual variations in weather, seasons and ingredients. Composting happens more quickly in summer, when there is a higher proportion of green material available.

Is it better to have an open heap or an enclosed bin?

Compost can be made successfully in either open or closed heaps, though most small gardens, with occasional ingredients, will benefit from a closed bin to keep warmth in.

Small plastic bins are good, sitting on soil preferably but not necessarily, and old pallets tied at their corners make good enclosures for larger gardens. Beware of expensive metal or plastic drums that swivel or rotate: they are often too sealed, allowing insufficient air to enter while they are being turned, so the ingredients are mixed without oxygen to feed the important bacteria.

What are green and brown ingredients?

Green ingredients are sappy, fresh leaves, trimmings and plants; *brown* ingredients are dead or dry organic matter and any soil on plant roots. Greens and animal excretions have more nitrogen, and browns have more carbon: some of each results in structured, nutritious compost.

Tomato seeds survive composting and I let them grow on this year-old compost heap as a cover.

What are the best ingredients?

Good results come from a mix of green and brown additions which, together, are moist without being soggy. Few gardens have the perfect combination – about six parts green to four parts brown – available at all times, so compost quality and the time needed to make it are always variable.

What can be used?

Any plant matter, fresh, dry or processed. So you can add weeds, including roots of perennials, and diseased materials such as blighted tomato plants (but see 'Special cases' below); vegetable and fruit peelings including citrus; paper (preferably crumpled) and non-shiny cardboard; animal manure; wood ash; vacuum cleaner bags except when they contain plastic; and soil in small amounts only. I advise breaking or cutting any larger ingredients into lengths of no more than 10–15cm (4–6in).

What can't be composted?

Plastic, metal, glass, thick pieces of wood, large stems, evergreen leaves and seeding weed heads. Disposable cups made of corn starch can be added, but they take a long time to rot.

How worthwhile is a shredder?

Chopped materials compost more quickly, so mechanical shredders are useful for large gardens and where a lot of woody material is to be composted. In most domestic situations they are not needed and I manage a large garden without one. You can use a rotary lawnmower to chop up fibrous ingredients.

SPECIAL CASES

- Large amounts of pernicious roots such as bindweed can be composted, but preferably in a light-proof bin and with enough other material to speed up their decay before they can grow again.
- Weeds with viable seeds are better burnt, because few domestic compost heaps attain enough heat (around 65°C/150°F – hot enough to burn the skin) to kill them. This problem will lessen as your garden becomes cleaner of weeds and fewer are close to seeding when cleared.
- Seeds of some garden flowers or herbs, such as forget-me-not, foxglove, pot marigold and feverfew, often survive composting. Although these plants are less noxious than many weeds, their sheer number means some extra hoeing will be needed when they emerge as tiny seedlings.
- Most diseased leaves can be safely added, including those infected with blight and mildew; and vegetables with pest damage (and the pests!) are safe to compost. But alliums infected with white rot around their roots, and onions with neck rot are best burnt.
- Large amounts of leaves are better piled in a separate heap, where they will turn brown and fibrous after at least a year. Nutrient levels in pure leafmould are not high unless some animal manure can be mixed with it, to add nitrogen to its carbon.

Do ingredients need to be layered or mixed?

Making layers of different ingredients is often advised, but this applies only when you are adding a lot of one green material such as grass mowings or weeds, which compost much better when alternated with something brown such as crumpled paper. This stops the green ingredients from packing into an airless lump, and provides the brown ones with enough nitrogen to break down.

Why is air so important?

Oxygen is an absolutely vital ingredient. Too much green at one time, squashing out the air, causes sogginess and smelly putrefaction instead of warm, sweet decomposition. Bacteria do a lot of the work initially and they need oxygen to multiply, which is why compost can be made extremely fast when the heap is regularly turned to admit fresh air.

Do heaps have to be turned?

If you have time to wait for compost to mature – about one year – then turning is not necessary. Heaps that are turned once, about a month after the final ingredients were added, develop into more even and sweeter-smelling compost, partly because of the mixing and partly because of bacteria being fed by the newly introduced air.

Can compost be made without a heap being hot at any stage?

Absolutely yes, but it takes more time and the process is more fungal, as opposed to bacterial. After about a year of occasional inputs, heaps should contain, at the bottom, some finished compost of high quality, whose extra fungi are a great health tonic for all soils.

Is one heap enough?

One bin is sufficient for a small garden if your inputs never reach the top. Keep adding new material for up to a year, by which time the bottom part will be ready to use.

Conical, 'beehive' bins are suitable for slow filling and occasional emptying. When there is some mature compost at the bottom, rather than trying to extract it from the door

Compost at different stages of decomposition: the current heap is at the back, the oldest compost at the front under cardboard.

at ground level, you can lift off the bin and place it alongside, then fork the top layer of partially decomposed material back inside to finish composting, remove the mature compost and carry on using the bin as before: see illustrations opposite.

What if the heap or bin never reaches full?

This is not a problem. It just means you will have less compost to use. The bin can still be emptied annually, as above.

Is an activator needed?

I have tried several proprietary activators, without noticing a significant difference to the composting process. Adding some animal manure or urine is the cheapest and most effective way of ensuring healthy composting; poultry manure is a most valuable ingredient, better composted than spread in a fresh state.

Is watering necessary?

Extra moisture is required only in hot summers when half or more of the ingredients are dry rather than soft and sappy. More problems are caused by a heap being too wet than too dry, so when watering dry ingredients, use a fine rose to water small amounts that are evenly dispersed.

Does a heap need covering?

Covers and lids are good for retaining heat and moisture, and also for excluding excess rainfall, especially on finished heaps when they are maturing. A plastic sheet is cheap and easy to remove and reuse; cardboard also works well, but modern carpets contain too many nasty chemicals.

How long before compost is ready?

Be patient. One year from start to finish is sufficient time for most of a heap to be usable; or if a heap is turned, compost can be ready in six months. Heaps made in spring and summer mature more quickly than heaps assembled in autumn and winter, partly because of higher ambient temperature, and also because many warm-weather ingredients are green rather than brown, which decompose more quickly.

When can a heap be used?

Good compost is dark brown, soft, moist but not soggy, more or less crumbly and pleasant smelling. When most of a heap is at this stage of decomposition, probably with some red brandlings (worms) at the bottom, I would use it, while forking any less decomposed ingredients into a new heap.

Does mature compost always contain worms?

Red brandling worms appear without being added and love to eat semi-mature compost; they excrete a finished product of smaller volume and of incredible value to soil and plants. Compost can also be used before they arrive, in a slightly less mature state. Brandlings (*Oesinia foetida*) live in soil but are not earth workers in the same way as earthworms (*Lumbricus terrestris*), which are fatter and longer and live mostly in soil, often at considerable depth.

What if compost is sodden and smelly?

Too much moisture and too little air leads to putrefaction. This means that you have

LIFTING A BIN TO SPREAD COMPOST

1 Lifting the plastic bin off the heap. The dog is smelling rats.

2 Forking the undecomposed top layer into a bucket, to be re-composted.

3 Filling a barrow with compost from the lower heap.

4 The soil after removal of the compost, with plenty of worms.

added a lot more green than brown; or too much rain has entered the heap; or there is poor drainage in the soil at its base. A remedy is to turn the whole heap to reintroduce air, cover it and leave it for two months in summer or half a year in winter, before spreading it on the soil. Or mushy compost can be spread in autumn: then, over the months before sowing and planting, air can enter and help it to break down.

What if it is dry and fibrous?

Introducing moisture evenly is not easy because water simply tends to run through a dry heap. I suggest watering lightly every day for a week, with a fine rose; or turning the heap and watering gently in stages as you move it.

How can rats be excluded?

Compost heaps are rats' ideal homes, offering food and warmth; even when food is reduced, they may still be resident. Enclosed bins of metal or plastic can be an answer but they exclude almost all air. At Lower Farm we are obliged to accept rats' presence and manage to co-exist, although they go foraging and eat more of the hens' grain than I would like.

IDEAS FOR BEDS AND PATHS
CREATING AND FILLING BEDS

What kind of bed?

When creating beds, it is often assumed that some kinds of wooden or plastic sides are needed, but this is not so: good vegetables can be grown on beds without sides and also on level ground.

Beds with sides
ADVANTAGES

- Where space is limited, raised beds yield more vegetables because of their depth of growing medium – preferably plenty of good compost.
- They reduce the amount of bending downwards needed and can be raised higher for those who have trouble reaching down.
- Beds offer a clear definition of growing areas, which is useful when plots are shared.
- Just one or two beds are an excellent way for beginners to learn vegetable growing.
- Paths in between may be mulched with membrane, wood chips or gravel, meaning no dirty feet.

DISADVANTAGES

- The cost of materials with which to create and fill them, and the time needed for this.
- Some extra watering is needed, especially for beds with wooden and high sides.
- Slugs and woodlice may inhabit the

Summer growth spills on to pathways and vegetables root into the path soil in search of nutrients and moisture.

spaces between sides and the bed, causing problems with seedlings and small plants.

Beds without sides

Not having sides and ends avoids much time and expense. This method is especially suitable for larger plots and allotments, and works well in my gardens. Comparing growth of vegetables on these beds with a handful of wooden-sided beds, I notice little difference, except for less slug and woodlice damage in open beds.

The advantages are much the same as for beds with sides. A major difference is that beds are less raised, especially by late spring when hungry birds are looking for worms in the surface compost, kicking some of it into pathways. This actually helps to keep the paths fertile and well structured for walking on. Also, beds that are less high conserve more moisture. The profile of beds in my garden is gently undulating rather than one of horizontals and verticals.

Growing on level ground

Having no beds, marking out rows as needed and then walking between them is a third way which often follows the digging of a whole plot, when all trace of previous rows and paths is lost: widely spaced vegetables such as potatoes and Brussels sprouts are suitable for this approach. However, the emphasis of this course is towards growing higher-value vegetables in a more intensive way, and this is most effective on beds.

Siting, creating and filling no-dig beds

Some of the many methods of creating beds are explained here. You can purchase kits of bed sides, but they are expensive. I recommend making your own where possible, or not using sides at all, to have extra money for the resource that really makes plants grow: compost.

Bed location

As long as water can drain away, beds may be sited anywhere that is reasonably level. Placing them on grass, gravel or even on paving stones without concrete grout are all fine, but soil underneath, which may initially be undug lawn or weeds, gives best results.

On sloping ground, I find it best to orientate beds down the slope and not across it. This makes watering and compost spreading easier, with less tendency for added materials to spill over the lower edges. On flat ground, as long as access to paths is not impeded, orient beds north–south so that sunlight is shared between all crops of different heights.

When materials are all to hand, beds can be simple and quick to make. See the illustrations opposite for ideas.

Edges

If you are making beds with sides, the most viable and natural material is wood. I recommend that you purchase untreated wooden planks, or scavenge old ones, and then paint on a product such as OSMO's 'clear oil wood finish', which is free of synthetic chemicals (see page 200).

Wooden sides can be 2.5–5cm (1–2in) thick. Thicker is better for durability and for straightness of long edges, but I caution against using sleepers: their extra thickness makes it harder to reach the middle of beds, and they also mostly contain creosote, which may seep out.

15cm (6in) planks make a deep enough bed for all vegetables: beds of greater depth may not improve growth significantly and require a lot of extra ingredients. The wooden sides of deeper beds are best lined with polythene on the inside, to retain moisture. Most people find widths of 1–1.2m (3–4ft) work well for access from both sides.

Plastic is sometimes used as edging, but it is only available in kit form. Its advantage over wood is that it allows better retention of moisture; this can also prevent overheating of dry bed sides in the summer. But there is some uncertainty over how long it endures without flexing or becoming brittle.

I do not recommend bricks and stones, because they are heavier to handle and harbour too many slugs.

Two ideas for wooden beds 15cm (6in) deep

BED 1 One way to create wooden beds is by hammering four 30cm (12in) lengths of 5 × 5cm (2 × 2in) square posts at each corner of your proposed bed, about 10–12cm (4–5in) into the soil. Check beforehand that the bed corners are square by measuring each diagonal to the same length. If they are different, adjust the corners and also re-check that the sides' and ends' length correspond to those of your prepared timber.

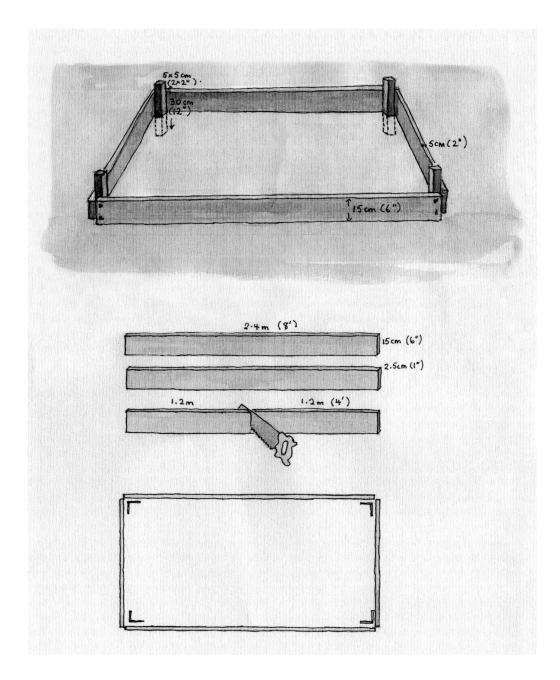

Bed sides are assembled by screwing or nailing four lengths of timber to the outside of four corner pegs (top drawing above). Extra pegs for the mid point of the sides' outer edges will be needed if planks are longer than 1.2m (4ft) or thinner than 5cm (2in), to prevent the wood from bowing out under pressure of the weight of compost inside.

MAKING A RAISED BED

1 Manure is simply placed on grass and weeds. Cardboard under the edges helps kill any couch grass. The last side is screwed on before the final filling.

2 After treading down the manure, I spread a last load of fine compost on top. The bed is now ready for sowing and planting (see page 95).

BED 2 (See bottom drawing, page 89.) A simpler idea, which you can adapt to the size of your plot. For each bed of 2.4 × 1.2m (8 × 4ft), buy three lengths of 2.4m (8ft) wood, 15cm (6in) wide and 2.5cm (1in) thick. Two of the planks are for sides, and the third one is sawn in half to provide the ends. They can be screwed together at the four corners using 90-degree braces, either inside or outside.

Then simply lay this frame in position and fill it as suggested below. There is *no need* to prepare the ground in any way, because the depth of organic matter will be enough to kill most green growth. But thinner coverings of organic matter, say 5–7cm (2–3in), will need a light-excluding mulch on top, such as cardboard (see page 52).

Contents

After the expense and trouble of assembling a bed, it is worth putting something richer than soil inside it and I would avoid purchased 'topsoil' of dubious quality. Even if it was good soil when scraped off, much of its value is then lost by stacking in heaps, which suffocates soil organisms.

I find that animal manure and compost give more vigorous and generally healthier plants. All organic matter should be reasonably well rotted, with lumpy ingredients at the bottom and the finest-quality compost spread as a top layer of 2.5–5cm (1–2in).

I do not prescribe exact ingredients, because organic matter is heavy and expensive to transport, so what you use will depend on what is available locally. For larger projects of several beds, you need to buy in bulk rather than in expensive sacks: a bed of 1.2 × 2.4m (4 × 8ft) contains just under a half ton of ingredients, depending how wet they are. To find a good deal, seek advice from local gardeners and allotmenteers, bearing in mind the advice in chapter 7.

Filling beds

The contents of a 15cm (6in) deep bed will be sufficient to smother the attempted regrowth of grass and weeds – though you will probably need to pull out the odd perennial weed that manages to poke through, in a much weakened state.

All the contents should be firmed down, so that plants have a roothold and the bed retains moisture, and to increase the quantity of the ingredients. Walking on a bed's contents is the best way to firm them and would hurt only if they were saturated with water. If the ingredients are wet, I walk on a plank to press them down, in order to spread my weight.

A good final profile is slightly domed upwards, the middle about 10cm (4in) higher than the edges, because even after being well trodden, the contents will be settling downwards for months afterwards.

Subsequent maintenance

With a bed filled this way, no digging or cultivation of any kind is necessary. It should be easy to keep weeds almost to zero, by pulling out any little ones as soon as they are visible, and they will slide easily out of the soft surface.

After a year of cropping it will take another 2.5–5cm (1–2in) of compost to keep the bed as full as it was. You need to repeat this every year, preferably in autumn, or when there is clear space.

Paths

Paths offer as much chance to be creative as the beds they surround. I suggest a width between adjacent beds of 45cm (18in), for general access, and a little wider for beds with sides if a wheelbarrow is to pass between.

Paths for beds without sides

Weeds are an issue for many pathways. The golden rule with paths, as much as with beds, is to clean them in a first year of light-excluding mulch, as described in chapter 5. If you allow perennial weeds such as couch grass to grow in paths, they will gradually colonize the adjacent beds.

Once the path soil is clean, I find it good to cover it, just once, with 5cm (2in) of basic compost such as green waste or composted bark, as long as it can be sourced cheaply. These composts are weed free, make weeding and hoeing easier, and improve the path's fertility, which benefits the vegetables growing in beds on either side. A once-only mulching and composting of paths is enough; then just keep them clean at all times.

I do not recommend gravel for paths, because it ultimately gets mixed into the soil, chiefly through worms casting above it. It may look pretty and discourage slugs for a while, but eventually you have a gravely soil, for ever, unless you also use a plastic membrane under the gravel, in which roots become entangled. I have similar reservations about wood chips and feel there is a danger of over-elaborating path coverings.

Other possibilities include leaves, straw and cardboard or paper, whose mulching properties will keep weeds down and conserve moisture. But light-excluding mulches afford shelter for slugs, whereas compost does not.

Paths for beds with sides

There are more options for paths of beds with sides because wooden sides are an effective barrier to the passage of annual plants, so it is feasible to have grass, for instance, as long as it is kept short. However, perennial weeds can still be invasive, especially if you do not regularly cut the paths.

I suggest a general mulch before creating beds, to clear all weeds. Then mulch paths between the beds with compost, wood chips or bark, and hoe or pull out all weeds you see.

LEFT Creating a slightly raised bed by scraping 5–7cm (2–3in) of soil from the path.

RIGHT January: spreading compost on beds. I have left leek trimmings for worms to pull down.

Possible harvests from beds

With some practice at sowing and planting, doing some plant raising to increase the season of growth (see chapter 10) and some replanting in summer, beds with fertile ingredients can be extremely productive. To give you some ideas about what you could grow in the space you have available, here are a range of harvests that I have achieved in different years.

Succession of vegetables from one bed

In 2006, from one bed of 1.2 × 6m (4 × 20ft) without sides, I picked vegetables as in the table below, from sowings and plantings between February and September. I divided the bed into eight lengths, A to H, of 75cm (30in). Each length had a first

MONTHLY HARVESTS FROM EIGHT SECTIONS OF A 1.2 X 6M (4 X 20FT) BED										
Vegetable	Apr	May	Jun	Jul	Aug	Sep	Oct	Nov	Dec	Total kg
A Pea, sugar snap			0.9	3.9						4.8
A* Radicchio							1.7	1.6		3.3
B Potato		0.2	4.0							4.2
B* Leek								1.5	1.1	2.6
C Onion				3.0						3.0
C* Kale						0.4	0.6	0.6	0.5	2.1
D Beetroot		0.3	3.7	1.8						5.8
D* Sugarloaf chicory							1.1	1.7		2.8
E Carrot		0.1	1.5	1.3						2.9
E* Beetroot						0.5	1.2	1.7		3.4
F Lettuce, leaf	0.3	1.7	1.8	0.3	0.3					4.4
F* Endive							4.4			4.4
G Spinach	0.8	1.8								2.6
G* Bulb fennel				2.1	1.1		1.2			4.4
G* Pak choi						0.8				0.8
H Garlic				1.7						1.7
H* French beans						3.5	0.4			3.9
TOTAL kg	1.1	4.1	11.9	12.4	3.1	5.2	10.6	7.1	1.6	57.1

sowing or planting, followed in summer by a second planting, denoted by asterisks. For example, from section H I harvested garlic (also the only overwintered vegetable here, planted in October) in early July; then I set out module-raised French bean plants, from a sowing on 29 June, where the garlic had grown (H*) on 14 July.

The year 2006 was a warm one and all the plants grew well, with some extra watering at times in summer. These figures are an indication of what can be harvested in different months, and of what vegetables to grow as first and second crops; see also chapter 12.

Year-round salad leaves from a small bed

In 2007 I grew salad of all kinds on one bed of 1.2 × 2.4m (4 × 8ft) with wooden sides,

starting in March with a planting of module-raised lettuce, spinach, chard and coriander and a sowing of peas for shoots. I sowed and planted more salads at different times through the year, including sorrel and spring onions in spring, and then oriental leaves, rocket, lamb's lettuce, chicory and endive in summer, keeping the bed reasonably full at all times.

First harvests in mid-April were 500g weekly, soon rising to 1–1.5kg from May to July, then 1kg weekly until mid-September, 500g weekly until late October and small amounts until year's end. More leaves then grew in March from overwintered plants such as lamb's lettuce and mizuna. The year's total was 35kg of leaves, equal to 280 salad packs of 125g each.

Early October. Four weeks after the bed was made (see page 90), autumn salads are growing vigorously.

MONTHLY HARVESTS FROM ONE 1.5 X 2.5M (5 X 8½FT) BED									
Vegetable	Apr	May	Jun	Jul	Aug	Sep	Oct	Nov	Total kg
A Onion					6.6				6.6
A* Leaf radish							0.8	0.3	1.1
B Beetroot		0.2	1.3						1.5
B* French beans				0.2	0.6	0.7			1.5
C Leeks								3.4	3.4
D Celeriac								5.2	5.2
E Pea, sugar snap		1.0	7.1						8.1
E* Radicchio						0.5	1.0	0.3	1.8
TOTALS kg		1.2	8.4	0.2	7.2	1.2	1.8	9.2	29.2

MONTHLY HARVESTS FROM ONE 1.5 X 2.5M (5 X 8½FT) BED									
Vegetable	Apr	May	Jun	Jul	Aug	Sep	Oct	Nov	Total kg
A Early potato			2.4						2.4
A* Endive, leaf						1.4	1.0		2.4
B Spinach		5.6	3.9						9.5
B* French beans					0.8	0.4			1.2
C Lettuce, leaf	0.7	3.1	3.6	0.6					8.0
C* Kale						0.8	2.2	1.0	4.0
D Parsnip 'Tender & True'								6.8	6.8
D Radish	0.4	0.2							0.6
E Parsnip 'Gladiator'								9.7	9.7
TOTALS kg	1.1	8.9	9.9	0.6	0.8	2.6	3.2	17.5	44.6

A year of harvests from one of the experiment's beds

In 2010, my experimental beds entered their fourth season and I offer here a record of that year's harvests from one of the undug beds, which measures 1.5 × 2.5m (5 × 8½ft) (see also chapter 2).

I had spread 2.5–5cm (1–2in) of well-rotted cow manure on the bed in November 2009. In late March 2010 I planted it with module-raised onions, beetroot and sugar peas, and then covered it with fleece for one month. In mid-May I planted the remaining space with celeriac and leeks.

After harvesting the onions, beetroot and peas, I planted leaf radish, French beans and chicory for salad leaves, so the bed was completely full until the end of September, when the beans finished. The leeks were attacked by leek moth, which reduced their yield, but they recovered enough to offer a fair harvest. There were just four plants of celeriac, which had grown large thanks to being watered in summer.

The uneven monthly totals are misleading because I stored the large harvests of onions and celeriac, for eating until April. The only glut was of peas in early July; I froze a few. Last harvests were in November and I then spread 2.5–5cm (1–2in) of home-made compost on the bed.

Different vegetables from the other part of the experiment

The bottom table (left) shows the harvests from the other undug bed in my experiment, of the same size, on which I had spread home-made compost in late November 2009.

In March I planted lettuce and potatoes, and at the same time sowed spinach, parsnips, and radish between the parsnips. I covered the whole bed with fleece for a month from the middle of March.

I gathered the radish over four weeks from late April and it finished before the parsnips grew too large. I then thinned the parsnips to fifteen per row and they grew so large that it was difficult to lever them out. Quality was excellent, with no forking.

The potatoes were disappointing because of a late frost on 12 May, which penetrated their cover of fleece. But this frost did no harm to the lettuce and spinach, which maintained a steady output for many weeks.

Autumn harvests were small but steady. I sowed kale in early June and planted it on 18 July as soon as the last lettuce was rising to flower and had been pulled to compost. I picked the outer leaves from the endive, as I did the lettuce, in order to have little and often for salads.

After the last harvests in late November, I spread well-rotted cow manure on the bed.

Carrots were sown the following April and the final harvest was in early September. See also page 199.

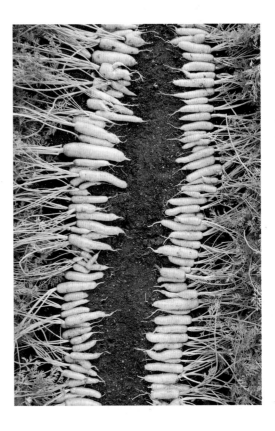

SEEDS AND RAISING PLANTS UNDER COVER
CONTAINERS, COMPOSTS AND METHODS

Seeds are like people. Some just leap into life with a wild desire to grow; others need gentle coaxing in a more sheltered environment.

You can often sow seeds direct – straight into the soil, *in situ* – as described on pages 114 and 143, and this is possible for many of the vegetables for which I give sowing advice in later chapters. You can also, however, set out plants. Plants are like mature teenagers who have been through the trickiest part of their lives and have reached a stage when they are able to face the world. Whether you raise plants at home or buy them in, there is often more guarantee of a fair harvest from plants than from seeds sown *in situ*. Also, in cooler climates and for certain vegetables such as tomatoes, we need to sow seeds before conditions are really right for them, to allow sufficient time for a harvest, and raising plants under cover allows us to do this.

Using plants saves a lot of time, space and seeds in the garden because the early stage of growing from seed, which is *much the slowest*, can take place in a surprisingly small space (seedlings take up little room) and you can offer those precious seeds ideal conditions, so that most of them succeed. The seedlings' early growth often seems infinitesimally slow, until a changeover point where they suddenly become larger, stronger and ready to plant.

You can have plants ready to put in the soil at any time you like, including in summer, after you have already taken a harvest of early vegetables. Second sowings and plantings allow many extra harvests and also translate into a smaller, neater, more manageable plot which produces the same amount to eat as a larger, less cropped and more weedy one.

It is therefore useful to create an indoor propagating area, where hundreds of seedlings can grow into healthy plants, while the soil is cold and empty in winter or while other vegetables are maturing outside. To give you an idea of the possibilities in a small area, in my greenhouse of 4 × 3m (13 × 10ft) I grow about 8,000 plants every year. Most plots could be filled with a twentieth of that. How to manage a small space for raising plants, what equipment you need and a few useful skills to learn, such as pricking out seedlings, are all discussed here.

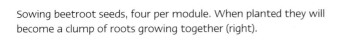

Sowing beetroot seeds, four per module. When planted they will become a clump of roots growing together (right).

Seeds

Seed freshness

When it comes to buying seed, there are plenty of choices, but of variable quality. A particular problem is that when we buy seed, we have no way of knowing its age. Sometimes this is unimportant, but in cases when it matters, especially parsnip and beets, whole sowings, much time and even an entire harvest can be lost. This has happened to me more often than I would like.

I have asked many in the seed trade for assurances on seed freshness, not always successfully, and have experienced poor germination of seed from no fewer than seven of the companies I buy from, in trials comparing their seed with other batches. When informed, they reply that germination was above the mandatory level when the seeds were last tested.

However, there is a clear difference between the 'germination' of a seed radicle – the first shoot to grow out of the seed – whose growth may subsequently peter out, and normal growth of the kind we need in our gardens. The latter happens when seed is reasonably fresh, although for some vegetables seed can be viable when older.

The figures given below are the longest recommended time for keeping seed, from their time of harvest. Numbers are based partly on my experience and partly on the advice of Real Seeds (see page 200).

KEEPING SEED	
Beans	3–5 years
Beets and chard	2 years; older seed grows more slowly
Cabbage family	3–7 years
Carrot	2–3 years
Courgette, squash	2–3 years; older seed is almost useless
Cucumber, melon	6–8 years
Lettuce	2–4 years; a marked decline in vigour after two years
Onion, salad onion, leek	2 years; then viability declines quickly
Parsnip	1–2 years
Pea	at least 4 years, possibly longer
Pepper, aubergine	3 years
Tomato	5–8 years

Seed needs to be kept in a dry state. Coolness helps too, but dry is the most important factor. Home saved seed keeps well in old envelopes or food containers; avoid polythene bags which trap any residual moisture.

A difficulty is that these figures mask the main problem of bought seed: we know only its date of purchase and packaging, rather than its date of harvest, which would have been *at least a year earlier*. After saving some seed, sow it alongside some bought seed to compare the growth.

Rubbing out seeds from a lettuce plant that was allowed to flower in summer.

Seed saving: a few tips

Saving your own is a great way of ensuring good germination, although it requires extra space in the garden as well as time and a little homework, to find out the different methods and timings for each vegetable. Real Seeds' website has much useful advice, and I offer some here, based on my own experience.

- A golden rule is not to save seed from F_1 hybrids, because it will 'out-grow' as different varieties, mostly undesirable. For some vegetables you need to be careful of cross pollination by insects, which may be carrying pollen of different varieties in your own or neighbours' plots.
- With biennials, save seed from plants in their second summer. *Biennial* describes a plant that grows for a year or part year, overwinters either in leaf (chard, kale, leek) or as a dormant root (parsnip, onion) before sending up a flowering stem in the spring, with seed drying through the summer. Do not save seed from, for example, chard or beetroot which have flowered ('bolted') in the same year as sowing, because the plants have not passed through a winter before flowering and therefore when sown the seed will be more likely to grow into bolters, rather than make chard leaves or beet roots.
- Peas are easy as long as you have space to allow a plant (or two), sown before the end of April, to remain unpicked and then

to stay in the ground until August, when its pods should be dry and crackling. Pick all the larger, well-formed pods, shell out the peas and keep them warm until you are sure that all seeds are fully dry and hard.

- Tomatoes, like peas, are simple, as they rarely cross pollinate, and offer seed as part of their harvest. Choose a healthy, good-sized, fully ripe fruit, cut out some of its seeds and wash them in water before drying on cardboard, which they will stick to and need gently prising off.

- Squash and courgette (not F_1 hybrid courgette) are examples of plants for which more care is needed to save seed to prevent it being an undesirable combination of different types of cucurbit. You need to choose and watch a healthy young courgette or squash fruit *before* its flower opens, rub a male flower of the same plant on the fruit's flower as soon as

it does open and then seal the flower with a paper bag held on with a rubber band, until the flower withers, so that it cannot receive any more pollen. Remember to mark the fruit and leave it unpicked until mature, and it should contain many seeds of the same variety.

- Lettuce needs one long season of steady growth, from a March or April sowing, to make a heart in June and July and then a flower bud, which needs staking when about 1m (39in) high; tufts of white seed will be ready to be rubbed out by September. Growing a plant under cover is a sure way of having seed by the end of August, and you should find that home-saved lettuce seed has noticeably more vigour than any you buy.

- Garlic is saved as bulbs rather than seed. Set aside the largest and healthiest at harvest time for planting its cloves in early autumn.

Different speeds of growth: wild rocket and land cress on the left, salad rocket and mustards on the right.

Raising plants under cover

Sowing seeds under cover or indoors – that is, in any structure which keeps rain off and accumulates some extra solar or other warmth – allows you enough control of temperature and moisture to ensure reliable growth of tender seedlings and young plants. In cool and wet weather, indoor plant raising is far easier than outdoor growing, and it helps you to fit many more plantings into soil that might otherwise be lying empty.

Higher temperatures are important in a high-latitude climate such as Britain's where the growing season is too short for certain vegetables, such as tomato, pepper and aubergine, to mature from an outdoor sowing.

Starting seeds in the warmth of a sunlit, sheltered space helps to bring forward the harvest of almost all vegetables, from courgettes, summer beans and beetroot to calabrese and cauliflower, so greatly extending the season of tasty vegetables for relatively little extra effort, once you have the basic materials to hand.

Windowsills

Often the most convenient place to start growth is beside a window, where seeds benefit from the ambient heat of indoors and often germinate quickly. However, windowsills are suitable only for germinating seeds and then for the first fortnight or so; after that levels of light are insufficient to support sturdy growth, which means seedlings grow into plants with longer, thinner stems and paler leaves than usual. Before this can

happen they need to go into a space with light from at least three sides, such as a cold frame or shelter attached to a house wall – many garden catalogues sell these.

Suitable structures and accessories

A walk-in structure such as a greenhouse or polytunnel makes an excellent propagating space: for options, see pages 35–6. You need some kind of shelving, and a small bench to work on, or a table outside the propagating space, for filling pots and trays and handling plants. To water, a small can with a fine rose is good, rather than expensive 'self-watering' accessories and capillary mats, which I rarely see working well. A final requirement is some containers for sowing and potting on: see 'Propagating trays' on page 36.

Other than these basic accessories, there is no need to buy the expensive and fancy gadgetry which is often called 'necessary', such as automatic ventilators for greenhouses – just leave the door or window open instead: ventilation is more important than keeping in that tiny extra bit of warmth.

Sowing and potting composts

Composts suitable for plant raising are free draining and have some nutrients added. You may wonder why nobody uses good soil from the garden. The reason is that plants raised in small pots or trays need *concentrated goodness*, in terms of nutrients, structure and water retention – more of each than is provided by soil.

Special 'seed compost' for sowing is the most free draining and has fewer nutrients than ordinary multipurpose compost, although the latter serves well for sowing most vegetable seeds, providing you take care not to overwater. Of vegetables, lettuce and basil need the most free-draining seed compost, because their roots suffer so quickly from even a hint of waterlogging.

Multipurpose compost for general plant raising is of varied quality. Avoidance of peat for environmental reasons means that new base ingredients are being developed, not always successfully, such as coconut coir, water industry waste, composted green waste and bark. The multipurpose organic compost I use for plant raising (see page 200) is based on peaty material that has been sieved out of reservoirs; it is light in weight, rich in nutrients and moisture retentive, and accommodates a high density of plant roots.

Should you have any spare, mature compost of your own, which is reasonably dry, you can use a large mesh sieve (1.5cm or ½in holes) to remove or break up any lumps larger than marbles, and then use it as a base for a potting compost by adding to each bucketful of compost about one-fifth sharp sand for drainage, and two handfuls of blood, fish and bonemeal.

When garden compost is of good quality – soft, crumbly and not slimy – I find it makes a dense and rich medium for plants; see 'A trial' on page 74.

The healthiest seedlings I ever observed were grown in pure and beautifully soft worm compost, but wormeries need much time to generate a useful amount of this precious resource. Mature home-made compost comes close in quality.

Sowing

Every vegetable has different-size seeds which come up at different speeds, with different requirements for moisture and temperature; do check the varied sowing suggestions I give in the next chapter.

Many small seeds can be sown as a clump in seed trays or small pots, for pricking out when they are small seedlings with just a couple of leaves (see page 109). Or you can sow seeds in twos and threes into modules or the smallest-size pots, for thinning to the strongest seedling. Some vegetables can be sown five or six seeds in modules or pots and then planted out as clumps of seedlings, without thinning: onions and beetroot, for example. Larger seeds such as peas, beans and sweetcorn can be sown into trays of larger modules, or small pots of 5cm (2in) diameter.

Sow seeds shallow rather than deep; they are better at pushing roots downwards than at pushing new stems up through lots of compost above them. A rule of thumb is to cover seeds with twice as much depth of compost as the seeds are thin (width not length); so most seeds need just a light sprinkling of compost, or a courgette seed of ½cm thickness needs 1cm (½in) of compost above it. Seeds of celery, celeriac and lettuce (see below) grow better for having light on them, without any covering of compost; use a sheet of glass over a seed tray instead.

I suggest that after filling your seed tray or module container, you water the compost thoroughly *before* sowing, then give only a light sprinkling after sowing, to avoid the risk of floating seeds out with the water.

The only seeds I do not sow indoors are carrot and parsnip, whose long taproots are easily damaged when seedlings

SOWING IN A MODULE TRAY

1 Use multipurpose compost to fill a sixty-hole module tray.

2 Spread the compost and then push it into the holes with your fingers.

3 After smoothing over, make shallow holes with your fingers.

4 Drop seeds into each hole and then scuff over to cover lightly.

are transplanted. However, you can successfully plant all other root vegetables such as swede and beetroot, from sowings in pots and modules.

Heating a propagating area

Heat is rarely necessary for most seedlings, but when frost-susceptible plants are growing some extra addition or retention of warmth is needed on sub-zero nights, mostly between March and early May. It is cheapest, simplest and often sufficient to lay fleece

and/or bubble wrap on such plants, each night frost is expected.

In larger structures it is useful to have electricity for providing extra warmth, such as an electrically heated propagation bench or heating mats. These are a more economical and time-saving way of giving heat to plants than space heaters of any kind.

Above all, don't even consider heating the air of a polytunnel, because polythene allows such a rapid escape of warmth: instead, its value lies in keeping wind off plants and in warming up internal air when there is brightness by day.

Watering

There really is no better option than doing the watering yourself, because all plants have different requirements for water. Each time you water is also an opportunity to see if growth is healthy, whether potting on or planting out is needed or fast-growing plants need spacing out, and whether slugs might be causing damage (see 'Pests' below).

Be careful to avoid overwatering recently sown seeds and small seedlings. Seeds sown in fully moistened compost need only occasional, light sprinklings until after their first true leaves are visible.

As seedlings grow into plants, their need for water increases steadily, especially in sunny weather, when roots are pumping moisture to feed growth in the leaves. It is good to be aware of the weather forecast, to water accordingly. Also I advise watering in the morning, so that plants are not cooled and left damp after watering in the evening; this can also encourage slugs, which slither hungrily by night.

The first visible leaves of most vegetable seedlings are a pair of cotyledons, followed by the first true leaf, which is more distinctively shaped and identifiable.

Pests in propagation

Keep propagating areas as clear as possible of damp habitats for slugs, such as large-leaved plants. Just one slug can eat a lot of seedlings, either chomping large holes in leaves or eating the whole plant almost to ground level. Should this occur, hunt for the culprit under seed and module trays, or scan the area with a torch as dusk deepens and molluscs emerge.

Staging with old wood encourages woodlice, which take tiny serrated nibbles from small leaves of spinach, tomato and cucumber mainly; they even nibble through the stems of tomato and cucumber. The best precaution is to thoroughly clean and sweep the propagating area in winter before you make any sowings. There is no need to use any chemicals; a simple brush serves well.

Mice often appear out of nowhere when peas, beans and sweetcorn are sown; they may also eat larger quantities of small seeds such as lettuce, even their leaves. I find it wise to set a mousetrap when sowing larger seeds, and also in late summer, when mice often enter a greenhouse to find something to supplement the decreasing amount of food outside.

Most vegetable plants survive freezing, even though they look miserable when frozen. Lettuce, spinach, peas, all brassicas, onions, beetroot and most herbs except basil are some of those that are frost hardy. Check the lists under 'Temperatures for sowing' on page 113.

Careful labelling of seed and plant trays is important!

SOWING AND PRICKING OUT LETTUCE

1 Sowing lettuce seed on seed compost in a seed tray.

2 Seedlings ready to be pricked out (lettuce and pak choi here).

3 Firming multipurpose compost into 2.5cm (1in) modules of a sixty-hole tray.

4 Lifting clumps of seedlings with their roots.

5 Pricking out lettuce into holes made by a pencil.

6 Pushing compost around a seedling's roots and stem.

Diseases

The most common is damping off, when small seedlings fall over and then rot, usually at cotyledon (two-leaf) stage. This is caused mainly by too much moisture, which causes fungal damage on leaves, stems and even roots. There is no remedy once it happens, but you can avoid it by taking care to sow seeds in their correct season (see chapters 11 and 12), by sowing more thinly so that air passes between stems, by watering seeds and seedlings infrequently, and by using free-draining seed compost, especially for lettuce and basil.

Pricking out

This means the transplanting of small seedlings, sometimes tiny ones. It is something of a lost art and deserves to be well learnt and adopted.

Pricking out is easier with tiny seedlings than small plants. The cotyledon stage is ideal, before any true leaf is visible, and the only tool you require is a pencil. Use it to 'dig' into the compost near the seedlings, and then underneath their roots, and lift them up in a clump to start with. Then tease them apart, holding them by a leaf, because leaves resist squashing much better than stems.

Seedlings can be put into already-filled module trays or small pots (no more than 5cm/2in diameter), with well-firmed compost that has been watered to full or nearly full moisture capacity.

Use the pencil to make quite deep, individual holes in each cell or pot, for as many seedlings as you want plants, discarding any weak or noticeably smaller ones. Holding them by their leaves, place

> Firm in the compost around seedlings pricked out into pots and trays, so that growing roots are well held. Roots don't have to point downwards: they can be pushed in willy-nilly.

each seedling into a hole so that *all its stem is covered with compost* and only the leaves are visible. This makes sturdy plants and they can send new roots off the buried stems.

Prick out a few more seedlings than you are likely to need for planting, in case of failures, and then compost unwanted seedlings, because there is no point in raising many more plants than you have room for.

Finally, lightly water the pricked-out seedlings. Then they often won't need water for a day or two afterwards, when they spend time settling in rather than growing.

Seedlings pricked out into a module tray, ready to grow.

Potting on tender plants

Most vegetables can be planted out at the size they reach in modules, plugs and small pots, often 5–7cm (2–3in) high and/or wide; for details of individual plants see chapters 11, 14 and 15.

A few vegetables that need extra warmth to grow are best potted on and kept in the propagating area until they are much larger: tomato plants, for example, need to be grown to about 20cm (8in) high and have a first truss of flowers starting to form before they are planted out.

Potting on or planting out are necessary when leaves turn a little yellow or blue and numerous roots emerge from holes in the base. You can tap or push out the root ball from below and gently push it into a premade hole in a slightly but not

I have often noticed that it works better to repot twice, each time into a slightly larger pot, than to repot once into a much larger pot, probably because it is easier to avoid overwatering in smaller pots. Perhaps plants also appreciate the extra attention and handling.

significantly larger pot of compost. Bury any long stems in the new compost to make the plants sturdier, and spread out the new pots to allow light from all sides. Then after two or three weeks, if it is still too early for final planting, you can move them again into a slightly larger pot.

Potting on: a small tomato plant growing in a 2.5cm (1in) module being put into a 5cm (2in) module.

Planting out

The ultimate act of all this propagation is setting plants in their final destination, a process that has three stages.

- *Hardening off* means setting trays and pots of plants outside, whatever the weather, for the plants to acclimatize for two or three days. No hardening off is needed when planting tender vegetables in an indoor space, or when planting outdoors under fleece and cloche.
- *Planting* involves making holes in the soil with a dibber for modules and plugs, or with a trowel for larger root balls, and pushing plants in firmly. All pot- and module-grown plants benefit from being pushed in a little below surface level. For plants with long stems, such as brassicas and tomatoes, make the holes deep enough so that you can bury the stem well, helping to make plants stronger.
- *Transition* happens for about a week after planting. During this time plants look a little fragile and growth is scarcely visible, although roots are forming undergound. Then suddenly a healthy lustre reappears in the leaves and new growth is rapid.

Module-grown plants ready to plant, of mizuna, red mustard and pak choi.

SOWING AND PLANTING
WHEN AND HOW, FOR BETTER GROWTH

This chapter is about sowing and planting methods, and dates, above all. Each date represents the assembly of valuable information about the growth of each vegetable I am recommending you to sow, and interlocks with many other pieces of the jigsaw to give you the best chance of success. Getting these right – for instance, by making sure you sow courgettes and summer beans at a time and in a place of sufficient warmth – leads to healthier growth.

I have grouped vegetables according to the part we harvest: leaf, fruit or root. Timings and methods of sowing and planting show consistency within each category, but there are important differences between them. Harvesting time also represents a key part of deciding when to sow them. Leaf vegetables have most flexibility in sowing dates, according to when you want them to produce, compared to fruit and some root vegetables, which are generally date specific, especially those that need a whole season to ripen their fruit or grow their roots. A fourth category is perennial vegetables, whose roots live for many years and which, when well established, produce harvests every spring and early summer.

The next three chapters explain all you need to know for successful sowing, while chapters 14 and 15 have more detail for the most popular vegetables about growing on to harvest.

Temperatures for sowing

Dividing the most grown, temperate-clime vegetables into three bands of temperature, according to their seeds' requirements for good germination and growth, it turns out that many in the cool category are grown for harvests of leaves, many in the medium category are vegetables grown for roots, and all the warm-category vegetables, basil excepted, are grown for fruits and seeds.

In the list below, 'cool' is approximately 5–12°C/41–54°F, equivalent to the temperature in March in a southern English greenhouse, in an average spring; 'medium' is approximately 10–20°C/50–68°F, or April

Planting dill in gaps between radish seedlings in early April.

indoors; and warm is approximately 18–30°C/64–86°F or the month of May indoors.

- **COOL**: brassicas, broad bean, carrot, lettuce, parsnip, pea, radish, sorrel, spinach
- **MEDIUM**: beetroot, celeriac, celery, chard, chervil, chicory, coriander, endive, fennel for bulb, onion, parsley, swede
- **WARM**: aubergine, basil, beans French and runner, courgette, cucumber, pepper, pumpkin, squash, sweetcorn, tomato

Almost all seeds in the cooler categories will germinate and grow at warmer temperatures, but the warm-category seeds will struggle to grow in cooler temperatures, except after being germinated in a warm place such as an airing cupboard.

All these vegetable plants tolerate some frost except for those in the warm category.

Terms explained

The descriptions below explain my use of certain words or phrases.

PLANT As described on page 22. Vegetables can be planted singly as several plants in a clump. This is useful for certain salads where you want smaller leaves; it also works for onions and beetroot. So don't automatically think of thinning modules to one plant before setting them out. I indicate where this can be done for certain vegetables: otherwise grow as single plants. 'Plant' in the lists below means outdoors unless otherwise specified.

SOW INDOORS Sow into seed trays, module trays and small pots, filled with compost, as described in chapter 10.

SOW DIRECT AND PLANT DIRECT For small seeds such as carrots, draw drills to a depth of 1–2.5cm (½–1in) in surface soil or compost, and sow about twice as many seeds as you want plants, so that after thinning the plants will be at the spacings indicated. For pea and bean seeds and tubers, dib holes at the spacings and plant at the depths suggested. Seeds need to be placed deeper when sown outdoors than when sown in modules.

SOW OUTDOORS To raise plants outside, draw drills as for sowing direct and sow seeds more thickly, every 1cm (½in), to grow a row with plenty of plants for setting out elsewhere. If making more than one drill, space them 25–30cm (10–12in) apart.

SPACINGS The figures I give are for healthy plants to make sufficient growth and yield the leaf, fruit or root we wish for; closer spacings can compromise the development of roots and fruits; wider spacings give larger harvests. Don't worry about exact spacing, but your harvests will be healthier and easier to gather when you follow the guidelines given here.

WEEKS This is the average time needed from sowing seeds to planting out. Longer times will be needed for early sowings in cool weather.

Susie pulling leek plants and choosing the strongest to put in holes dibbed by Charles.

Vegetables for leaves

All the salad plants listed here are covered more fully in chapter 14.

Frost hardiness

All of these vegetables tolerate their leaves being frozen, apart from basil and summer purslane.

▼ Basil

WHERE/WHEN TO SOW
  Sow indoors April–June
TIME FROM SOWING TO PLANTING
  5–7 weeks
WHEN TO PLANT AND SPACING Late May–
  July in shelter, 20–30cm (8–12in)
TIPS Likes warmth, dislikes damp
Basil needs heat at all stages, and dry air to grow healthily. So it is never worth sowing outdoors in spring, and even in a greenhouse I wait until the middle of April.

Seed can be sown in a tray and pricked out: keep seedlings and small plants growing in gentle warmth and be careful to water sparingly. There is no rush to plant basil outside until summer is well under way, so plants usually need potting on before planting. Handle them carefully because they have fragile roots.

▼ Broccoli for heads in summer and autumn (calabrese)

WHERE/WHEN TO SOW Sow indoors or
  outdoors March–June
TIME FROM SOWING TO PLANTING 4 weeks
WHEN TO PLANT AND SPACING April–July,
  39–45cm (15–18in)
TIPS Cover with fleece or mesh if possible
Make early sowings in a small tray or pot to prick out, or sow two/three seeds per module and thin to the strongest. Early plantings can be covered with fleece after setting out, for about a month, to make heads of tender calabrese in June when vegetables are still scarce and even before butterflies are too numerous.

The year's final sowing date I recommend is late June, for planting by late July, preferably under a mesh cover against insects, to make heads in October and until winter arrives. Heads of calabrese survive autumnal frosts of −4°C/25°F or so.

LEFT Sweet basil in 2.5cm (1in) modules, ready to pot on.
RIGHT Calabrese, lettuce and purple cauliflower ready for planting out.

Broccoli for heads in spring (purple or white sprouting)

WHERE/WHEN TO SOW Sow indoors or
outdoors May–June

TIME FROM SOWING TO PLANTING 4 weeks

WHEN TO PLANT AND SPACING June–July,
45–60cm (18–24in)

TIPS May need cover of mesh or net
Sow seed as for calabrese, either in May for
really large plants, or in the first week of
June for planting in early July, which allows
a preceding harvest of spring salads, spinach
or garlic.

▼ Brussels sprouts

WHERE/WHEN TO SOW Sow indoors or
outdoors April–May

TIME FROM SOWING TO PLANTING
4–6 weeks

WHEN TO PLANT AND SPACING May–June,
60cm (24in).

Although they eventually grow large,
Brussels sprout plants take a while to get
underway and can be sown either in a small
row outdoors in April or indoors in May in a
seed tray or pot for pricking out.

Packets of hybrid varieties contain few
seeds and indoor sowing should ensure
they all grow, perhaps giving enough plants
from one seed packet. Prick seedlings into
modules or small pots, and then set plants in
their final position by the middle of June.

▼ Cabbage for autumn/winter hearting

WHERE/WHEN TO SOW Sow indoors or
outdoors May–early June

TIME FROM SOWING TO PLANTING
4–6 weeks

WHEN TO PLANT AND SPACING June–mid-
July, 45–50cm (18–20in)

Sow cabbage for autumn hearting in May
and for winter hearting (savoys mainly) in
early June. Seed is often of variable quality,
so I like to sow it in a pot or tray, and then
prick out only the strongest seedlings; or
plant only the strongest plants from an
outdoor row.

The red cabbage and Brussels
sprouts plants on the left are
ready for planting. The kale
and broccoli plants on the
right need about ten days to
grow some more.

Cabbage for spring leaves and hearting

WHERE/WHEN TO SOW Sow indoors or
   outdoors mid- to late August
TIME FROM SOWING TO PLANTING
   4–5 weeks
WHEN TO PLANT AND SPACING Second half
   of September, 20cm (8in) for leaves and
   40cm (16in) for hearts

Sow as for autumn and winter cabbage
above. Plants need to be in the soil before
the end of September, so that they have time
to establish before winter.

Cauliflower

WHERE/WHEN TO SOW Sow outdoors
   March to early June, indoors February–
   June
TIME FROM SOWING TO PLANTING 4 weeks
WHEN/WHERE TO PLANT April–July
SPACING 45–60cm (18–24in)

Make March/April sowings and plantings
as for broccoli (calabrese), to have curds in
June and early July. May sowings are more
at risk of caterpillar damage in late summer
and autumn.

Then in June you can sow certain varieties
to stand the winter and make curds in spring,
but be prepared for a struggle to protect
them against pigeons in winter.

▼ Celery

WHERE/WHEN TO SOW Sow indoors
   April–June
TIME FROM SOWING TO PLANTING 6 weeks
WHEN TO PLANT AND SPACING May–July,
   30cm (12in)
TIPS Sowing too early causes bolting

Celery seed is tiny and needs light to
germinate, any time from April to early
June. Sprinkle a little seed on top of moist
compost in a seed tray or pot, cover with
glass and keep in a warm place with light,
but preferably not full sun. Tiny-leaved
seedlings should appear after about two
weeks and can be pricked out as soon as you
are able to handle them.

After another month you should have
small plants which can be set out, any time
from late May until July, in soil which has
plenty of organic matter to hold moisture for
celery's thirsty roots.

Celery grows slowly and is
ready to plant when small, as
shown by extensive roots.

Chard

WHERE/WHEN TO SOW Sow direct or indoors late April–July

TIME FROM SOWING TO PLANTING 3–4 weeks

WHEN TO PLANT AND SPACING May–August, 10–40cm (4–16in) for small or large leaves

TIPS Sow late August–early September for indoor winter leaves

Although chard germinates in cool conditions, it is best sown in warmer weather, because if young plants are exposed to too many shorter days and cool nights, they may flower at some point in summer.

Seeds are large; each one can grow two or three plants, and chard grows well in such clumps. Sow any time until July; direct sowings need to be thinned to the desired spacing, according to whether you want larger or smaller leaves.

Chinese cabbage for hearting

WHERE/WHEN TO SOW Sow indoors July

TIME FROM SOWING TO PLANTING 3 weeks

WHEN TO PLANT AND SPACING August, 30cm (12in)

A lovely vegetable but prone to insect damage, and the most successful harvests come from sowing at exactly the right time. Sow in the last week of July for plants to grow in the warmth and moisture of late summer and autumn and heart in October.

Seedlings grow faster than almost any other. Either sow two seeds per module or small pot, for thinning to the strongest, or sow in a tray and prick out after four to six days. Plants will be ready to go out within three weeks.

Chervil

WHERE/WHEN TO SOW Sow direct or indoors, July–August

TIME FROM SOWING TO PLANTING 4 weeks

WHEN TO PLANT AND SPACING August–September, 10–20cm (4–8in); later plantings can be indoors for winter leaves at 20cm (8in)

Most seed packets advise sowing chervil at any time in spring and summer, but I have found that spring sowing gives minimal harvests before plants flower, whereas summer sowing results in bushy, long-lived plants which produce an abundance of healthy leaves throughout the autumn.

Seed is small and can be direct sown, for thinning out after three to four weeks, or can be sown indoors in pots or modules, aiming for one to three seedlings in each, for planting as a clump.

Chicory for forcing

WHERE/WHEN TO SOW Sow direct or indoors mid-May–early June

TIME FROM SOWING TO PLANTING 3–4 weeks

WHEN TO PLANT AND SPACING By end June, 30–39cm (12–15in)

These plants need a whole season of growth but there is a risk of flowering if they are sown too early. One option is a late-May sowing in modules or pots indoors, with two seeds thinned to one plant; this allows you tomake an earlier sowing of spinach or radish and plant out the chicory in the same place after you have harvested them in late June. Plants grow large by autumn, with bulky roots to harvest before Christmas for forcing indoors.

Chicory for hearts

WHERE/WHEN TO SOW Sow indoors June–
25 July

TIME FROM SOWING TO PLANTING
3–4 weeks

WHEN TO PLANT AND SPACING July–mid-
August, 30–35cm (12–14in)

Chicory is more likely to flower than to heart
if sown in April, May and even early June.
Plants from a July sowing, set out in August,
can follow a harvest of onion, carrot and so
forth, making them a most useful second
crop vegetable for autumn and winter salads.
Sow and prick out as for endive hearts below.

Chicory for leaves

WHERE/WHEN TO SOW Sow direct or
indoors June–August

TIME FROM SOWING TO PLANTING
3–4 weeks

WHEN TO PLANT AND SPACING Late June–
August, 10–20cm (4–8in)

TIPS Sow late August–early September for
indoor winter leaves.

Best sown direct as the seeds germinate
easily and can be grown closer than hearting
chicory, even in clumps; or sow as for
endive hearts.

Coriander

WHERE/WHEN TO SOW Sow indoors April
or direct July–August, 'Calypso' variety

TIME FROM SOWING TO PLANTING 4 weeks

WHEN TO PLANT AND SPACING August–
September, 15–20cm (6–8in); later
plantings can be indoors for winter leaves

As with chervil, coriander flowers readily
when sown in spring and early summer, but
not before some leaves are produced, and
the dry seeds of late summer are edible too.

Biggest leaf harvests come from July sowings
for picking through autumn, and August
sowings to stand the winter.

Seed is large enough to handle easily and
can be sown direct, or two seeds per module
or pot, and thinned to the strongest.

Lamb's lettuce/corn salad

WHERE/WHEN TO SOW For winter leaves,
best sown direct late August

SPACING Thin to 5–10cm (2–4in)

Probably the hardiest outdoor winter salad,
from well-timed sowings. If sown before
mid-August, plants mature in October and
November and are at risk of mildew. Late-
August sowings stand the most chance of
reaching a fair size as well as staying healthy
over winter.

For direct sowing, draw out drills quite
close together, about 15–20cm (6–8in), sow
seeds about 2.5cm (1in) apart and thin after
a month if necessary. Unless your soil is clean
you will need to weed carefully, because
germination is slow and in weedy soils you
risk seeing the small plants smothered.

Endive for hearts

WHERE/WHEN TO SOW Sow indoors
June–July

TIME FROM SOWING TO PLANTING
3–4 weeks

WHEN TO PLANT AND SPACING July–
August, 30–35cm (12–14in)

One of the easier seeds to germinate, and
only a few plants are needed, but beware of
slugs in the fortnight after setting out young
plants. Seedlings grow well after being
pricked out, so I sow clumps of seeds in a
pot or tray for pricking into modules or small
pots. A most underrated autumn salad.

Endive for leaves

WHERE/WHEN TO SOW Sow direct or indoors June–August

TIME FROM SOWING TO PLANTING 3–4 weeks

WHEN TO PLANT AND SPACING June–September, 20–25cm (8–10in)

TIPS Sow late August–early September for indoor winter leaves

Similar to hearting endive but spacing can be closer and the sowing season continues until late August, when sowings are for plants to harvest through winter, preferably under cover.

Kale

WHERE/WHEN TO SOW Sow direct or indoors May–June

TIME FROM SOWING TO PLANTING 4 weeks

WHEN TO PLANT AND SPACING June–July, 40–50cm (16–20in)

Timing of sowing is similar to that for purple sprouting and savoy cabbage, so they can all be sown together in a seed tray and then pricked out into carefully labelled pots or modules. Planting needs to be deep and firm, with a good dose of water if dry. Plants often need protection with net or mesh, against birds and insects.

Land cress

WHERE/WHEN TO SOW Sow direct or indoors late July–August

TIME FROM SOWING TO PLANTING 3–4 weeks

WHEN TO PLANT AND SPACING August–early September, 20cm (8in)

TIPS Sow late August for indoor winter leaves

Land cress flowers in May, so spring sowings make few leaves before flowering; most benefit comes from sowing and planting in August, for autumn salad. Seed is small; be careful to sow thinly, either direct or into modules, and thin to one plant.

Leaf beet spinach

WHERE/WHEN TO SOW Sow direct or indoors April–July

TIME FROM SOWING TO PLANTING 4 weeks

WHEN TO PLANT AND SPACING May–August, 22–40cm (9–16in) for small or large leaves

TIPS Sow August–September for indoor winter leaves.

Leaf beet is a tough plant and once established it can provide leaves for many months, although they are most tender when plants are young, so a sowing in April and again in July works well, also in August for covering with a cloche over winter. Pull or cut out any plants that rise to flower.

Leek (see also chapter 15)

WHERE/WHEN TO SOW Sow outdoors April or indoors March–April

TIME FROM SOWING TO PLANTING 5 weeks (indoors) and 8–10 weeks (outdoors

WHEN TO PLANT AND SPACING May–mid-July, 15cm (6in) or 10 × 30cm (4 × 12in)

Leek seedlings look like grass and grow slowly, but like onions they are nutrient hungry and need a large module or pot for indoor sowing, with four or five seeds in each. Plant these as a clump, unthinned, to have plenty of medium-size leeks; they will have a long, tender stem and little whiteness, because they are planted only just below soil level.

Outdoor plants can be lifted with a trowel and separated out. Discard all the small ones, and then plant individually with roots 7–10cm

(3–4in) deep, so that the lower part of the stem becomes white and sweeter. Use a dibber to make individual holes for each plant, knock some surface soil or compost back into the holes on top of the leek roots, and water gently so that the plants don't float out.

Lettuce for hearts

WHERE/WHEN TO SOW Sow direct from March, or indoors February–July

TIME FROM SOWING TO PLANTING 4 weeks

WHEN TO PLANT AND SPACING April–early August, 22–30cm (9–12in)

TIPS Sow in late August for plants to overwinter and heart in the spring

Use the sowing guidelines for lettuce for leaves below; the only difference is a slightly wider spacing and an earlier last sowing date.

Lettuce for leaves

WHERE/WHEN TO SOW Sow direct from March, or indoors February–August

TIME FROM SOWING TO PLANTING 4–6 weeks

WHEN TO PLANT AND SPACING April–August, 20–22cm (8–9in)

TIPS Sow early September for indoor winter leaves.

Lettuce seed is small and light and grows best when left uncovered. Indoor sowings can be in a tray or pots of moist compost, and then covered with glass or a polythene bag for up to a week, by which time roots will be developing and first leaves visible. Speed of growth is closely related to freshness of seed.

Outdoor sowings need covering with soil, but only a little, and watering every five days or so in dry weather; after four to six weeks, plants can be thinned when they are still small but perhaps large enough to eat. For more detail on this productive and varied salad, see chapter 14.

Lettuce in 3cm (1in) modules ready to plant. Left to right: 'Grenoble Red', 'Chartwell', 'Rosemoor', 'Red Sails' and 'Freckles'.

Onions for salad

WHERE/WHEN TO SOW Sow direct March–
June or indoors January–June
TIME FROM SOWING TO PLANTING
4–6 weeks
WHEN TO PLANT AND SPACING April–July,
5–20cm (2–8in)
TIPS Sow late August for plants to stand
winter and harvest in the spring
When sowing direct, expect to do some careful
weeding around the slow-growing seedlings.
Make sure you use fresh seed and if sowing
indoors in summer, germinate the seeds out
of direct sun, as they lie dormant when too
warm. I sow eight seeds per module to have
clumps of five or six onions in each. Onions are
exceptionally hardy and survive winter as small
plants about 7cm (3in) high, often looking
rather straggly but then bursting into healthy
growth in March and April.

Oriental leaves and rocket

WHERE/WHEN TO SOW Sow direct or
indoors July–August (early August is best)
TIME FROM SOWING TO PLANTING
2–3 weeks

These parsley plants could be potted on or
planted out.

WHEN TO PLANT AND SPACING August–
early September, 15–22cm (6–9in)
TIPS Sow mid- to late September for indoor
winter leaves
All these widely varied plants need to be
sown after midsummer, to avoid their
spring flowering season. I find that July
sowings suffer from pests such as flea
beetle and caterpillars more than August
sowings, which are better placed to enjoy
the dampness of autumn. Sowings in the
first two weeks of August give the most
productive harvests, and I restrict sowings
in late August to the fastest-growing plants
– mizuna, leaf radish, 'Green in the Snow'
mustard and salad rocket.

Wild rocket is an exception, much slower
growing and slower to flower, so I sow it in
July for autumn and spring harvests.

All these seeds can be sown in modules
with two to four seeds, depending how many
plants you want in a clump; fewer plants means
larger leaves. Sowing direct is straightforward,
with satisfyingly rapid germination, and failures
should be rare because these seeds stay viable
for several years.

◄ Parsley

WHERE/WHEN TO SOW Sow direct March–
July, or indoors February–July
TIME FROM SOWING TO PLANTING
6–8 weeks
WHEN TO PLANT AND SPACING
April–August, 22cm (9in); later plantings
can be indoors for winter leaves
Parsley germinates and grows slowly at first,
even in summer. Seed can be sown as early as
February, perhaps in a pot on the windowsill.
Flat-leaved parsley germinates and grows a
little more quickly than curly-leaved, but also

flowers more readily, so it is a good idea to sow some of each seed.

▸ Peas for shoots

WHERE/WHEN TO SOW Sow direct March–
June or indoors February–June
TIME FROM SOWING TO PLANTING
2–4 weeks
WHEN TO PLANT AND SPACING March–July,
20–30cm (8–12in)

Once you master the knack of picking them, pea shoots become an easy and delicious addition to salads. Seeds maintain their viability for many years and can be saved at home: see page 100. For early shoots I sow three seeds in each module or small pot indoors in March, harden them off when 5cm (2in) high by leaving plants outside for three or four days, and then plant out as clumps and cover with fleece. Peas are hardy and survive frost and snow, but fleece helps them to establish more quickly.

Choose seed of a tall-growing variety (to 2m/6ft) so that shoots are longer and more vigorous. *Spring sowings are the most productive*, with plentiful harvests possible in May and June. Sowings in June and July make smaller amounts of leaf and shoot before they want to flower (flowers are delicious) and also they are at risk of mildew on leaves.

Purslane, summer

WHERE/WHEN TO SOW Sow direct June–
July or a tiny pinch of seeds per module
TIME FROM SOWING TO PLANTING
3–4 weeks
WHEN TO PLANT AND SPACING
15–22cm (6–9in)

A difficult vegetable unless summer is dry: it is worth making a small sowing in any

Peas for shoots being planted between lettuces 'Fristina' (left) and 'Mottistone' (right).

spare soil and seeing what grows. In hot weather when other salads are flagging, this one is ebullient – indeed it is a weed in many tropical areas and is known as pigweed in North America.

Rocket: *see oriental leaves*

Sorrel, broad-leaved

WHERE/WHEN TO SOW Sow direct March–
July or indoors February–July
TIME FROM SOWING TO PLANTING
4–6 weeks
WHEN TO PLANT AND SPACING March–
August, 25–30cm (10–12in). Later
plantings can be indoors for winter leaves.

Sorrel is perennial and may survive many years. You can start a clump or two from roots sliced off an existing plant in winter (slide a sharp trowel or spade down its edge) or from sowing a few of the tiny seeds. Sowing is a useful way of having plants to grow indoors in winter, from sowings into modules or small pots in August, to plant under cover by the end of September as a clump of three or four seedlings.

Spinach

WHERE/WHEN TO SOW Sow direct March–April and then July, or indoors February–April and then late July

TIME FROM SOWING TO PLANTING 3–4 weeks

WHEN TO PLANT AND SPACING April and August, 15–22cm (6–9in)

TIPS Sow early September for indoor winter leaves

Two good periods for sowing are early spring, so that plants have time to make plenty of leaf before their summer flowering, and late summer for plants to stand the winter. Spinach grows equally well from either direct or indoor sowings; the latter are easier to keep free of nibbles by slugs, birds and woodlice. I aim to use seed less than two years old, sow three or four seeds per module or small pot and plant as a clump. See also tree spinach on page 175.

Winter purslane

WHERE/WHEN TO SOW Sow direct or indoors, early to mid-August

TIME FROM SOWING TO PLANTING 4 weeks

WHEN TO PLANT AND SPACING By mid-September, 15–22cm (6–9in)

TIPS Sow mid-September for indoor winter leaves

A great standby for mild-flavoured winter leaves, from sowings in late summer. Growing wild in damp, mild areas it was a valuable source of winter and spring vitamin C for miners in the Californian gold rush and the Cornish tin mines. I suggest using the two dates above, one for outdoor leaves in autumn and one for indoor leaves in winter. Seeds are tiny and it is easy to sow them too thickly, so it is worth thinning seedlings to two or three per module, for planting as a clump.

I explain how the indoor winter salad plants, seen here in March, have all survived being frozen many times.

Vegetables for fruits

Extra warmth

Most fruiting vegetables benefit from higher temperatures to raise healthy plants, especially in germinating their seed: see page 113. Also the vegetables listed in this section are killed by frost except for peas and broad beans.

Buying plants

Some of these plants require much time and heat to reach a stage where they can be planted early enough and at a worthwhile size, close to their flowering stage. If your propagation possibilities are limited, buying plants is a worthwhile option, especially for aubergines, peppers and tomatoes. They will probably arrive in April and need potting on, but the slowest bit is done and growth should then be rapid.

Frost-sensitive plants need warmth to make healthy growth, so early plantings outdoors, if conditions are cold, risk failing. Average, earliest planting dates are the middle of May in southern England, late May in northern England and early June in Scotland – if in doubt, ask your gardening neighbours. Don't be influenced by fellow allotmenteers, who may plant runner beans too early!

▸ Aubergine

WHERE/WHEN TO SOW Sow indoors in
   warmth 20–30°C/68–86°F February–
   March

TIME FROM SOW TO PLANT 8–12 weeks

WHEN/WHERE TO PLANT AND SPACING
   Plant May indoors/June outdoors,
   45cm (18in)

TIPS Heat loving

Except in hot summers on sunny patios in southern England, aubergines need to be grown indoors. Plants will be healthier and larger when warmth is provided, resulting in earlier harvests.

Aubergine in the polytunnel, with begonias for colour and pleasure.

125

French beans ready to plant out. I sowed two seeds per module and thinned to the strongest.

Beans, broad (see also chapter 15)
AUTUMN
WHERE/WHEN TO SOW Sow direct late October–early November, 5 × 39cm (2 × 15in), dib holes 5cm (2in) deep or draw a drill of that depth
TIPS Net against birds pulling seedlings
SPRING
Sow direct February–May, or indoors January–May
TIME FROM SOW TO PLANT 3–6 weeks
WHEN/WHERE TO PLANT AND SPACING March–May, 10 × 37cm (4 × 15in)
Broad beans often grow better from direct sowing than from planting. Spacings for autumn sowing are closer to allow for losses through winter, but surviving plants then make new stems (tillers) in spring, so gaps fill up in April and May.

Beans, dwarf French
(see also chapter 15)
WHERE/WHEN TO SOW Sow direct June or indoors May–June
TIME FROM SOW TO PLANT 2–3 weeks

WHEN/WHERE TO PLANT AND SPACING May–July, 30–39cm (12–15in)
Sowing in April is possible but healthier plants are more likely when you wait for warmer conditions in May, for sowing indoors, or early June for outdoor sowing. A last sowing in late June should provide plenty of beans in September and even October if mild.

Sow in trays of large modules or in small pots, and you can set them out when still small, 5–7cm (2–3in) high, rather than potting on to make large plants.

▲ Beans, runner and climbing French (see also chapter 15)
WHERE/WHEN TO SOW Sow direct early June or indoors May–June
TIME FROM SOW TO PLANT 2–3 weeks
WHEN/WHERE TO PLANT AND SPACING Late May–early July, 30cm (12in) with 1.5–1.8m (60–72in) between double rows
Sow indoors as for dwarf beans above, but eventual spacing is wider and plants take longer to start bearing than dwarf beans.

Courgette, marrow, pumpkin, squash (see also chapter 15)

WHERE/WHEN TO SOW Sow indoors mid-April–May, pot on if sown in modules

TIME FROM SOW TO PLANT 4–5 weeks

WHEN/WHERE TO PLANT AND SPACING
Mid-May (fleeced) or late May–June, 60–100cm (24–39in)

TIPS Can be sown outdoors in late May to early June

The leaves are extremely frost sensitive, so April sowings need to be indoors and benefit from extra warmth. Sow in modules or small pots, and then transplant into larger pots after two or three weeks, usually when a first true leaf is developing. If it is at all cold when planting out, cover with fleece for about a fortnight to help plants establish.

Squash for winter such as 'Red Kuri', 'Crown Prince' and especially 'Butternut' need every possible growing day to mature their fruit, so are best sown indoors by the end of April, for planting out in May or, at the latest, in the first ten days of June.

Cucumber

WHERE/WHEN TO SOW Sow indoors in warmth (20–30°C/68–86°F), April–May, pot on to have large plants after 5–6 weeks

WHEN/WHERE TO PLANT AND SPACING
May–June indoors, or sow outdoors early June, 75–90cm (30–36in)

Plants thrive in warmth and are extremely fragile; take care, because seed of hybrids is often expensive, but worth the expense for more productive indoor growing. Sow in modules or small pots filled with seed compost for better drainage, because roots of young plants are susceptible to any slight waterlogging. Pot on when the first true leaf is developing, handle more gently than tomatoes and water plants sparingly.

▼ Melon

WHERE/WHEN TO SOW Sow indoors in warmth (20–30°C/68–86°F), March, pot on to have large plants after 8–10 weeks

WHEN/WHERE TO PLANT AND SPACING
May–early June indoors, 75–90cm (30–36in)

Melons need warmth and a long season to succeed; ripe fruit in August and September will be testament to much skill and careful adherence to the timings given above. Use the same procedure as for cucumbers, except for sowing a month earlier.

Melons on one plant of 'Sweetheart' F1 in the polytunnel in late August. The stem is wrapped around string.

Pea (see also chapter 15)

WHERE/WHEN TO SOW Sow direct April–May, either in dibbed holes 2.5cm (1in) deep or a drill of that depth; or sow indoors March–early May

TIME FROM SOW TO PLANT 3 weeks

WHEN/WHERE TO PLANT AND SPACING April–May, 10–15 × 60–150cm (4–6 × 24–60in)

TIPS Survives frost

Make March sowings indoors in modules or small pots; after planting out, these thrive under a fleece cover, which can also be used over direct outdoor sowings. I sow two or three seeds per module and transplant without thinning at the spacings above: the wider spacing is for tall varieties of pea, growing to a height of 2m (6½ft).

▼ Pepper, sweet and chilli

WHERE/WHEN TO SOW Sow indoors in warmth (20–30°C/68–86°F), February–March

TIME FROM SOW TO PLANT 8–12 weeks

WHEN/WHERE TO PLANT AND SPACING May indoors/June outdoors, 45cm (18in)

TIPS Heat loving

Similar to aubergine but a little less demanding of heat. Chilli plants in particular should manage to bear fruit outdoors in a sheltered position, in as much sun as possible.

Grown in the polytunnel these 'Diablo' peppers have ripened well. They were sown in March and are shown here in early October.

Sweetcorn (see also chapter 15)

WHERE/WHEN TO SOW Sow direct May–
early June, or indoors mid-April–May
TIME FROM SOW TO PLANT 2–3 weeks
WHEN/WHERE TO PLANT AND SPACING
May–July, 30–37cm (12–15in)
Indoor plantings in mid- to late April grow
well in modules, but beware mice eating the
seeds; I prime a trap when sowing them.
When sowing and planting outdoors, wait
until about the middle of May, when all risk
of frost has passed.

Tomato (see also chapter 15)

WHERE/WHEN TO SOW Sow indoors
in warmth (20–30°C/68–86°F), late
February–March
TIME FROM SOW TO PLANT 8–12 weeks
WHEN/WHERE TO PLANT AND SPACING
May indoors and June outdoors, 45–
60cm (18–24in)
Tomatoes have similar requirements to
aubergine and pepper in terms of needing
warmth and a long season of growth. But
tomato plants tolerate cooler conditions,
once seeds have germinated at 20–30°C/68–
86°F. For more sowing details, see page 196.

Vegetables for roots

Many of these vegetables can be raised
indoors and transplanted outdoors (unless
otherwise specified), with some or all of the
following benefits:

- earlier harvests, especially of beetroot,
  which can be ready by early June
- more reliable growth, for instance, of
  swede seedlings, which often struggle

against insects when sown directly in soil
- bigger harvests, especially of onions and
  celeriac.

Of roots that are grown from seed, I sow
only carrot and parsnip direct. Of roots
grown from tubers, cloves and sets, I plant
them all direct in the soil.

Frost hardiness

All these vegetables can stand being frozen
to a greater or lesser degree, apart from
potatoes.

Artichoke, Chinese

WHERE/WHEN TO PLANT Plant tubers direct
April or indoors March–April
TIME FROM SOW TO PLANT 4 weeks
WHEN/WHERE TO PLANT AND SPACING
April–May, 45cm (18in)
It is often advised that artichoke plants are
frost sensitive, but they are in fact hardy
and tubers even survive the winter in soil,
except in extreme cold. April is the best
month for planting tubers direct, with a
dibber or trowel at 7–10cm (3–4in) deep.
Unfortunately they grow in number rather
than size, which makes them slow to harvest:
experiment with a couple of plants to see
how you manage.

Artichoke, Jerusalem

WHERE/WHEN TO PLANT Plant tubers direct
March–April, 45–60cm (18–24in).
Easy to grow and difficult to stop growing
from tubers left in the ground after harvest.
Plant tubers any time in early spring as for
Chinese artichokes. Suitable for making a
summer hedge up to 2.3m (7½ft) high.

Beetroot 'Boltardy' in June. I sowed four seeds per module indoors in March, planted in April and fleeced the plants for one month.

▲ Beetroot

EARLY

WHERE/WHEN TO SOW Sow direct mid-April or indoors March–April

TIME FROM SOW TO PLANT 4–5 weeks

WHEN/WHERE TO PLANT AND SPACING April–May, 7 × 30cm (3 × 12in) for direct sowings, and 30–39cm (12–15in) for multi-sown modules

FOR WINTER

WHERE/WHEN TO SOW Sow direct or in modules June

TIME FROM SOW TO PLANT 3–4 weeks

WHEN/WHERE TO PLANT AND SPACING June–mid-July, spacing as above

Beetroot is easy to transplant, the only difference from direct-sown plants being that roots have more than one thin root coming out at the bottom of their swollen globe. For early harvests I recommend 'Boltardy' as the least likely to flower, and it has tasty roots of deep red. For sowing in May and June, the varietal choice is wider and includes white and yellow roots; see 'Second sowing' on page 143.

Sow three or four seeds in modules or small pots and thin to four or five seedlings (some seeds germinate more than one seedling), transplant when true leaves are developing and cover April plantings with fleece for two weeks or more.

▶ Carrot (see also chapter 15)

EARLY

WHERE/WHEN TO SOW Sow direct, late March–April, 2–3 seeds per cm (5–7 per inch) in rows of 30cm (12in), thin after a

Carrots can be covered with mesh or fleece at this stage – recently thinned – or earlier.

month to one seedling per cm
(2 per inch)

FOR WINTER ROOTS

WHERE/WHEN TO SOW Sow direct mid-
June ideally, 2 seeds per cm (5 per inch)
in rows of 25–30cm (10–12in), thin after
a month to 1 seedling per cm (2 per inch)
or less if you want really large carrots

Early April is often a good time for first
sowings, when the soil has warmed a little
and slugs are therefore less likely to eat
seedlings. Tiny, thin leaves should be visible
within ten days, but stay small for a month.
If they don't appear, slugs have probably
eaten them and re-sowing is needed.

A fleece covering helps early growth, and
also protects against rabbits and carrot root
fly, when left on until harvest time.

Celeriac

WHERE/WHEN TO SOW Sow indoors in
March with warmth if possible, in a seed
tray for pricking out after three weeks

TIME FROM SOW TO PLANT 8 weeks

WHEN/WHERE TO PLANT AND SPACING
Mid-May–early June, 39–53cm (15–21in)

Celeriac benefits from some extra warmth
at sowing time and from remaining
unfrozen at any stage while a seedling, as
low temperatures induce plants to flower
in late summer. However, sowing early in a
warm seed tray, around the middle of March
and by early April at the latest, offers more
chance of achieving good-sized roots.

Seeds are tiny: sow them in fine compost
and leave uncovered, with glass or a plastic
bag on top, to retain moisture and warmth.

After about three weeks there should be plenty of small seedlings to prick out into modules, and they need to be grown on under cover for another four or five weeks before being hardened off to plant out. In cold springs covering plants with fleece for two or three weeks helps them establish.

Fennel, bulb

WHERE/WHEN TO SOW Sow direct or indoors, June–early July

TIME FROM SOW TO PLANT 3–4 weeks

WHEN/WHERE TO PLANT AND SPACING Late June–early August, 25–30cm (10–12in)

Fennel for bulbs is often sown too early in spring, resulting in thin bulbs which rise to flower before fattening up. I find that sowing from about 10 June until 10 July is most reliable: it is late enough for plants to bulb rather than flower, and early enough for plants to have time to develop good-sized bulbs.

Sow two or three seeds in modules or small pots, thinning to one plant in each after about ten days when the tiny, feathery seedlings are showing a small true leaf; then plant out after another fortnight or so.

Slugs adore small fennel, which consequently disappears fast in wet conditions. Plant in your most slug-free area, using your favourite precautions (see chapter 13) so that once plants are established, after a fortnight or so, growth can continue with few other problems.

Direct sowing is also possible, when soil is dry and slug free.

Garlic and elephant garlic

WHERE/WHEN TO PLANT Plant cloves direct late September to March (early plantings give larger harvests), 15cm (6in) in blocks or 10 × 30cm (4 × 12in) in rows

Autumn plantings allow garlic extra time to grow because, whether planted in autumn or early spring, it bulbs up in the lengthening daylight of early summer, for harvesting by early July. Plants are completely frost hardy. Break the bulbs into separate cloves and keep any small ones for eating. Use a dibber to make holes to push the cloves into, with their fatter end downwards and 2.5–5cm (1–2in) of soil above their tips. Or plant them less deep and spread compost or manure on the whole bed after planting.

Be patient when waiting for growth to be visible, as they put down a lot of roots first and sometimes you see no leaves until January, even February, from an October planting.

Kohl rabi

WHERE/WHEN TO SOW Sow direct or indoors, April–early August

TIME FROM SOW TO PLANT 3–4 weeks

WHEN/WHERE TO PLANT AND SPACING May–August, 30–39cm (12–15in)

I advise sowing in modules, two seeds thinned to one plant. Spring sowings need to be harvested before the roots are tennis-ball size; otherwise they turn woody, even though they look appetizing. Best results come from July sowings, which avoid spring flea beetles and bulb up through autumn.

'Sturon' onions in July. I sowed eight seeds per module indoors in February and planted them outside in early April.

▲ Onion and shallot

(see also chapter 15)

WHERE/WHEN TO SOW Sow seed direct in
  March or indoors February–March

TIME FROM SOW TO PLANT 4–6 weeks

WHEN/WHERE TO PLANT AND SPACING
  April–early May, 25cm (10in). Module
  plants or sets direct mid-March–mid-
  April, sets 12cm (5in) or 7 × 25cm
  (3 × 10in)

Onions from seed are slow to grow and
planting sets is easier. Use a dibber to make
holes and put the fatter end downwards,
sometimes with tiny roots just visible and
even a green shoot from the top as well.
Do not plant sets before the third week in
March, to avoid them bolting in May and
June, when you see a stem with a round
flower bud; if this happens, pull the onion
immediately and eat whatever is tender, as
there is no point in leaving it to flower.

However easy sets may be, they also risk
bringing disease into your plot, especially
mildew or neck rot: see pages 156–7. To
reduce the chances of this, sow seed of
mildew-resistant varieties in modules indoors
with six to ten seeds in each, thinned to the
five or six strongest plants after about three
weeks, and planted when still quite small,
without thinning. Onions actually like growing
together in clumps and their bulbs push one
another apart as they swell in early summer.

Parsnip

WHERE/WHEN TO SOW Sow direct
February–June, 2 seeds per 1cm (5 per
1in) in rows of 30cm (12in), thin after
two months to 5 × 30cm (2 × 12in)

Parsnip seed is slow to germinate and it helps
to sow a few radish seeds in the drill with it,
because the radishes' fast growth allows you
to see the line where parsnip seedlings will
emerge, which can take four weeks. Weed
carefully, pull the radishes when ready and
thin the parsnip seedlings at the same time.
Later sowings in May and June make smaller
roots and may need occasional watering of
the soil while seeds are germinating. If soil is
full of weed seeds, wait until they germinate
and then hoe off all growth before sowing.

Potatoes, first and
second early (see also chapter 15)

WHERE/WHEN TO PLANT Plant tubers
direct, late March–mid-April, 30–40cm
(12–16in)

TIPS Frost tender

Potatoes can be grown in large pots, say
25cm (10in) across, and if you have space
indoors this is a way of having really early
potatoes in May, from a February planting.
Set tubers about 5cm (2in) below the surface
and add some extra compost if small new
potatoes become visible at surface level.

Otherwise plant tubers (chitted with
sprouts or not) outside at the dates
given: there is no rush, because leaves are
vulnerable to late frost, so keep pulling earth
and compost over the new leaves until all
danger of frost has passed.

Potatoes, maincrop

WHERE/WHEN TO PLANT Plant tubers
direct, April–early May, 40–50cm
(16–20in)

TIPS Frost tender

The method is similar to that for early
potatoes but use a slightly wider spacing, and
there is less worry about frosts in s
pring, because of the later planting. On the
other hand, blight may cause difficulties:
see page 156.

> The next three roots, along with kohl
> rabi, are all brassicas and suffer the same
> pest issues: see chapter 13.

Radish

FOR SPRING AND SUMMER HARVEST
Sow direct March–May, thin after one
month to 1 × 25cm (½ × 10in)

FOR AUTUMN HARVEST
Sow direct late July–mid-August, thin after
three weeks to 5 × 30cm (2 × 12in)

Radish seed germinates fast and seedlings
usually need thinning because, if left too
thick, roots struggle to develop. For spring
sowing, use small red or red and white
varieties ('French Breakfast'); they can be
sown between or even in rows of slow-
germinating seedlings such as parsnips, or
around vegetables that are about to finish,
such as winter salads. For autumn harvests,
sow larger pink, black and white varieties
such as 'Minnowase'.

▼ Swede

WHERE/WHEN TO SOW Sow direct or
 indoors late May–early June
TIME FROM SOW TO PLANT 3–4 weeks
WHEN/WHERE TO PLANT AND SPACING
 Late June–early July, 30–35cm (12–14in)
Swede seedlings are often nibbled hard by
flea beetles when sown direct, so they are
healthier when grown indoors. Another
reason to sow them in modules or small
pots is that one module tray of forty plants
is quite enough for most plots. Sow two
or three seeds per module and thin to the
strongest. Cover the planting with mesh if
it is hot and dry in late June, to help plants
survive the summer insects. If sown direct,
they need thinning by early July. Roots
continue swelling until November.

Turnip

WHERE/WHEN TO SOW Sow direct or
 indoors July–mid-August
TIME FROM SOW TO PLANT 3 weeks
WHEN/WHERE TO PLANT AND SPACING
 August, 20–25cm (8–10in) for multi-
sown modules or thin after a month to 5 ×
 30cm (2 × 12in) for direct-sown roots
Although turnips can be sown in spring,
for eating as small roots before they flower,
their main season is autumn and at that
time they fit nicely into the vegetable plot
because of their rapid growth. This allows
them to be sown after many summer
vegetables have finished, such as onions and
early beans. Remember to thin young plants
because thick sowings, which initially look
magnificent, result in tiny turnips.

Swede 'Helenor'. Sown in modules three weeks earlier, two seeds per module, and thinned to the
strongest, it is now ready to plant.

Perennial vegetables

These vegetables need sowing and/or planting only once, for harvests over many years. However, they still need a fair amount of maintenance, such as weeding and tidying. It is important to plant into soil that has been cleaned of all perennial weeds, especially couch grass, because of the difficulty of removing such weeds once the vegetables are growing.

▶ Artichoke, globe

WHERE/WHEN TO SOW Sow indoors
March–April,
TIME FROM SOW TO PLANT 4–6 weeks
WHEN/WHERE TO PLANT AND SPACING
May, 75–90cm (30–36in)
TIPS Or plant roots in spring or autumn
An easy vegetable, which needs much space. Using a sharp spade to cut downwards into an existing plant gives new plants, from October to March.

▶▶ Asparagus

WHERE/WHEN TO SOW Sow indoors
March–April
TIME FROM SOW TO PLANT 8–10 weeks
with potting on
WHEN/WHERE TO PLANT AND SPACING
Summer, 90cm (36in)
TIPS Or plant purchased crowns March–
early April.
It is not difficult to grow asparagus plants from seed, but it adds a year to the two or three years you need to wait for a first harvest, compared to when you plant roots, which are called crowns. I sow in modules, discard any weaker plants and pot on after four weeks, or when roots are pushing

Globe artichokes in early summer. The plants are fourteen years old but die back every winter.

ROOT DIVISION OF PERENNIALS
You can propagate globe artichokes and rhubarb by using a sharp spade to slice some root(s) and a small part of the main stem off the edge of existing, well-established plants, preferably in late autumn, and planting them straightaway in clean soil where they are to grow.

Asparagus in August. Picking stopped six weeks earlier and the spears have grown into 2m (6½ft) ferns.

through the bottom. While these plants are growing, be sure to clean their planting patch of all weeds. Rather than using the ridges sometimes recommended, I plant on flat ground: harvests are good and weeding is easier.

Rhubarb

WHERE/WHEN TO SOW Sow indoors
   March–April
TIME FROM SOW TO PLANT 8–10 weeks
   with potting on
WHEN/WHERE TO PLANT AND SPACING
   Summer, 90cm (36in)

TIPS Or plant a piece of root in autumn, and
   before February

If a neighbour or friend has good rhubarb, they may be persuaded to let you slice a large root or two off their clump, any time from October until February, when rhubarb is most dormant.

Otherwise sow seeds in spring, as for asparagus, although they grow more quickly. After potting on and planting out by July, you may have good-sized plants by the following spring, allowing a light picking in their first season.

COMPANIONS AND SECOND CROPPING
GROWING TOGETHER, ROTATION AND SUCCEEDING WITH SUCCESSION

Vegetables of many kinds, and some annual flowers, can grow side by side and this chapter presents some ideas for combinations that accommodate the different spaces and timings required. There are also ideas for second cropping, or successional sowing, and suggestions for which vegetable sequences are good in a general way – a system called rotation.

Growing together and rotating

Vegetables as neighbours

It works better to keep small and large plants separate, especially in temperate climates, where light is important. This prevents shading of smaller leaves by larger ones, which may also offer a home to slugs, who will then have an easy passage to tender small plants.

For example, it works well to grow perennials such as rhubarb, globe artichokes and asparagus in one part of the garden or in one bed, and to group large annual vegetables together, separately from smaller salad plants, carrots, dwarf beans and bulb fennel. Second sowings and plantings of the small vegetables can then happen in clearer space with full light and moisture. Another factor is that vegetables such as climbing peas and beans pull moisture from a wide area on

The polytunnel in September. Small French marigolds complement the growth of tall, cordon tomatoes and are one factor in reducing aphids.

either side of their row, so they need some bare or mulched soil around them and no leafy vegetables growing too close.

Companion planting

This term is used for plants that grow better in close proximity. I have experimented with many of the classic combinations and still use a few, such as planting French marigolds beside indoor tomatoes. The marigolds discourage aphids, their pattern of growing – low and bushy compared to the tall tomatoes – is complementary, and they look nice together.

By contrast, I have twice grown carrots between rows of onions and salad onions, because the smell of onions is supposed to deter carrot root flies. Yet those carrots had as many maggots in them as any others in the garden at that time – whereas the onions were superb!

Certain suggestions for plant companions, while perhaps valid in certain combinations of soil and climate, may be invalid in others.

Probably the best method of companion planting is of a general rather than precise kind. Simply growing plants of many different

Vegetables that taste good together are often good companions while in growth: for example, tomatoes and basil, parsley and garlic, carrots and onion, lettuce and cucumber – see 'Intercropping' on page 142.

families, interspersed with some flowers, thus creating a range of habitats for wildlife, is an excellent path to plant health, and recreates every year a beautiful, enjoyable garden.

Longer and shorter periods of growth

The length of time between sowing and harvesting is extremely variable and knowing the differences can help to make a plot far

more productive. Many annual vegetables take only two or three months, occasionally four, from planting to harvest and can be preceded or followed by others, as in the examples at the end of this chapter.

However, some vegetables do need all or nearly all the growing season to reach a worthwhile size, or for their fruit to mature, or for continual cropping. Of these, the main ones are parsnip, Jerusalem artichoke, maincrop potato, chard and leaf beet, celeriac, courgette, sweetcorn, summer and winter squash, climbing beans and Brussels sprouts. There is scarcely enough time at either end of the season to grow another vegetable in the same space, although some intercropping may be possible, such as sweetcorn and squash (see page 142).

Requiring less than a whole season, but still the greater part of it, are certain cabbages, calabrese and cauliflower. But when sown early and harvested by July, these vegetables can be treated as the first part of a two-harvest year. Other vegetabless crop even more quickly: these are ideal for March or April sowings and early summer harvests. They include lettuce, spinach, peas, carrots, beetroot, shallots and early potatoes. For sowings to follow them, see page 144.

A third group of vegetables can be planted in late summer or autumn and stand the winter, with established roots that spring into early growth and give harvests in the hungry gap or soon afterwards. They include garlic, spring cabbage, broad bean, spinach and spring onion, and their time of growth gives great possibilities for second cropping.

Squash and sweetcorn are happy to share a bed (see page 142).

Rotation

I do not rotate crops in the traditional way, finding it better to grow what I need, leaving as long a gap as possible – *which may be only two years* – between vegetable families such as legumes, brassicas, potatoes, alliums and umbellifers. (Note that 'roots' are not a family, so counting them as a group makes no sense in terms of a rotation to avoid disease.)

You need to bear rotation in mind, without letting it dictate what you grow. There are several groups of vegetables with family associations. Within each group, plants are susceptible to similar pests and diseases, which can be reduced by growing vegetables of the same family in different places each year *as far as is practical.*

All gardeners have favourite crops and I know many who successfully ignore rotation altogether, for instance by growing carrots and runner beans in the same place every year or tomatoes in the same greenhouse soil each summer. When rotating minimally, adding compost and manure does help to keep soil, and therefore plants, in good health.

FAMILY: common name/Latin name*	VEGETABLES and common herbs
Alliums/Alliaceae	Chive, garlic, leek, onion, salad onion, shallot
Asparagaceae	Asparagus
Beets/Chenopodiaceae	Beetroot, chard, leaf beet, orach, spinach
Brassicas/Brassicaceae	Broccoli, Brussels sprout, cabbage, cauliflower, kohl rabi, land cress, oriental leaves, radish, rocket, swede, turnip
Cucurbits/Cucurbitaceae	Courgette, cucumber, melon, squash
Grass/Poaceae	Sweetcorn
Legumes/Fabaciae	Broad bean, French bean, runner bean, pea
Lettuces/Daisy/Asteraceae	Artichokes (globe and Jerusalem), chicory, endive, lettuce
Mint/Lamiaceae	Basil, Chinese artichoke, marjoram, mint, rosemary, sage, thyme
Polygonaceae	Rhubarb, sorrel
Solanums/Solanaceae	Aubergine, chilli, pepper, potato, tomato
Umbellifers/Umbelliferaceae	Carrot, celery, celeriac, chervil, coriander, dill, fennel, parsley, parsnip
Valerianaceae	Lamb's lettuce (corn salad)

* I have included more than one name where several are commonly used.

Vegetables not mentioned are winter purslane, related to claytonia wildflowers of North America, and summer purslane, which is related to wild moss roses.

Intercropping

It is sometimes possible to sow or plant between rows of a vegetable that has just been sown or planted at a wide spacing, or which is about to finish its growth. This gives you either an extra harvest or an extra month or so in which to achieve a second one, and is simple to manage when soil is clean of weeds. I have enjoyed success with all the following combinations, and there are more to try.

- Parsnips can be sown with a few radish seeds, about one radish every 5cm (2in): the radishes grow and mature before parsnip seedlings are of medium size. Also the fast-emerging radishes help to identify the row(s) of parsnip seeds before they come up. Radish can also be sown between rows of parsnips, a little more thickly, and both methods also work for sowings of carrots.
- Lettuce can be planted in late spring at the same time as, and between, kale or Brussels sprouts, which allows enough

Second plantings after carrot harvest: mustard 'Red Dragon', pak choi 'Baraku', pak choi 'Red Lady' and mustard 'Pizzo'.

time for lettuce hearts to grow before the brassicas cover them over; or you can pick the outer leaves of the lettuce for several weeks.

- Sweetcorn can be planted (this is better than sowing) in the gaps between winter squash. Plant both at the same time: two sweetcorn for each squash plant, set 1m (39in) apart.
- Carrots and beetroot can be sown between rows of maturing garlic in early June, by which time the garlic leaves will be starting to go yellow. Simply draw drills in the usual way, water them if dry (see 'Sowing in dry soil' opposite) and seedlings should be showing true leaves by the time you harvest the garlic bulbs. A variation on this is to plant parsley, beetroot, dwarf beans or swedes between the garlic in early to mid-June.
- Garlic can be grown with parsley under cover in winter: plant parsley in September at its usual spacing of 25–30cm (10–12in) and then plant garlic cloves between the small parsley plants in October. They will all survive winter together and you can pick parsley from February to May, then pull it out when rising to flower, leaving the garlic to mature in early July. I grow some enormous cloves this way, as garlic enjoys the extra warmth from being under cover.
- Tall, cordon tomatoes can be underplanted with small bush or Greek basil, which, although never able to grow abundantly in the tomatoes' shade, offers tasty leaves and probably helps the tomato plants to grow more healthily.
- I have also managed to grow lettuce under cucumbers: the lettuces are smaller than usual but of good quality.

Second cropping

What happens to growing areas after the early summer harvests of lettuce, spinach, broad beans, beetroot and so forth? If you can have some plants ready, a second harvest is often possible in the same space and this can be good for the plot, because fewer weeds grow when soil is cropped and there is more incentive to keep weeds at bay, which is of great long-term benefit.

To succeed with succession requires preparation and some precision about dates for sowing and planting, to make best use of diminishing daylight after midsummer. For some second vegetables, it helps to have raised plants in a propagating space (see chapter 10), for both spring and autumn cropping, so that three or four weeks of growing is already done before their roots even meet the soil.

Soil preparation between first and second vegetables

Preparing ground for a second planting or sowing is simple when there are few weeds. You just need to clear all surface remains of the first harvest, including any stems just below soil level, but leave all small roots in the soil.

After pulling out roots such as those of cabbage and lettuce, or harvesting garlic, soil is best trodden back down to leave it firm – don't be afraid of walking on undug soil, whose structure should easily take your weight. I find that vegetables grow fine after the soil is trodden down, which also helps to break surface lumps and conserve moisture.

If soil looks bare of compost, and also after a first harvest of cauliflower and calabrese, I spread a little (1cm/½in) crumbly compost before making a second planting. Or after a month or so, you can mulch the soil between second plantings, such as those of leeks and calabrese, using less-broken-down compost or manure (or fine compost if you have it!).

Sowing in dry soil

Sowing in summer is often in dry soil, and this can actually result in better germination than when soil is consistently wet, by using the following method.

Draw your drill or drills slightly deeper than usual, about 2–3cm (1in), and then run a watering can slowly along their length so that water fills the drill without overflowing its sides. If soil is really dry, it is good to do this two or three times.

The idea is for seeds to lie on this damp soil and send their roots down into it. Above them is dry soil, which you pull back over once the seeds are sown. 'Sow in dust, grow they must' – it looks dry, but there is moisture where it is really needed.

Avoid the temptation to water the soil at any stage for at least three weeks, until seedlings are established, and they should be troubled with fewer weeds and slugs than usual, because of the dry soil.

Watering

In dry weather, new plants need watering, precisely rather than massively. I find that using a long-handled dibber gives enough leverage to make reasonably deep holes in dry soil, with a slight hollow around each plant, making it possible to give small amounts of water where most needed, just around new plants and not over the whole area. Precise watering of sowings and plantings saves much water, and means fewer weeds grow.

Succeeding through the year

The table below gives ideas of vegetables that can be grown in the first half of the season, and of suitable vegetables to follow them. It is good to have a clear idea of which ones are good in each role.

The dates given are for sowing and planting, either direct or in pots or modules – for specific advice, see chapters 11 and 12. In this respect a table can be misleading; this one is to give an approximate framework.

SOW/ PLANT	FIRST VEGETABLE	SOW/ PLANT	SECOND VEGETABLE
Aug–Sep	Cabbage for spring	May–Jun	Beans (French and runner); many others
Mar–Apr	Spinach, radish	Jun	Almost any vegetable, such as swede, carrot, beans, celery
Oct–Nov	Garlic, broad bean	May–Jul	Kale, cabbage, calabrese
Mar–Apr	Early potato	Jun–Jul	Beans (French and runner), leek (sown April), brassicas
Mar–Apr	Lettuce, carrot, beetroot	Jun–Jul	Dwarf bean, leek, many salads
Mar–Apr	Cauliflower, calabrese, pea	Jul–Aug	Lettuce, endive, chicory
Feb–Apr	Onions	Jul–Aug	Endive, chicory, turnip
Mar–May	Many vegetables	Aug	Oriental leaves, spinach, chervil, coriander, parsley, endive

1 Early May: garlic and parsley overwintering in the polytunnel. The parsley is nearly flowering and finished.

2 Late June: the garlic has been harvested. I planted the melon a month earlier after removing the parsley.

A great skill to acquire is having plants ready for setting out soon after clearing the first vegetable, even on the same day. This saves up to four weeks of growing time and so effectively extends the season by that amount.

You can also make the growing season longer and increase harvests by covering March and April sowings and plantings with fleece or a cloche, just for a month or so, to propel the vegetables into abundant growth by May.

Many more combinations are possible, according to your climate, skills, facilities and preferences for harvests. I list examples some of my successions below.

FIRST PLANTING		SECOND PLANTING	
Onion	sown February,* planted March, harvest of 6.3kg early August, from 11 modules of 5 plants in each	Turnips	sown in early August and 3kg harvested by November, from two rows
Beetroot	sown February,* planted March, harvest of 3.1kg in June, from 5 modules of 4 plants in each	Leeks	April sowing outdoors, planted in late June, 3.2kg harvested by December, from 15 plants
Pea, tall sugar snap	sown and planted March, harvest of 8.5kg in late June and July, from 12 modules of 2 plants in each	Endive	module-sown July, planted early August, 1.6kg harvested by November, in several pickings of outer leaves from 5 plants
Lettuce	sown February,* planted March, harvest of 11.3kg April–July from 18 plants of 3 different varieties, their outer leaves picked weekly	Leeks	April sowing outdoors, planted mid-July and 3.3kg harvested by December, from 22 plants
Early potato	planted March, harvest of 4.3kg by mid-June from 4 tubers	Carrots	sown mid-June and 2.7kg harvested October from one row of 1.5m (5ft)
Spinach	sown March, 9.5kg harvested by early June from 2 rows of 1.5m (5ft)	Dwarf beans	planted in early July and 1.2kg harvested by September from four plants

*Grown in modules, with some warmth from a propagating bench to germinate seeds, in the greenhouse

Versatile vegetables

Some vegetables behave differently according to when they are sown. For example, spinach sown in March or April will rise to flower within two or three months, so it is ready to be cleared by June and can be followed by many summer and autumn vegetables.

On the other hand, when sown in early August spinach can live for nine months, giving leaves in autumn, surviving the winter and then providing leaves again until the end of May. So it can be used to precede or to follow. Similar examples of altered behaviour are offered by most plants that can survive a winter outdoors, such as overwintering varieties of cabbage, cauliflower, lettuce and onion.

Other vegetables are more predictable and offer a harvest after a half season as either first or second crops. They include beetroot, calabrese, carrot, kohl rabi, lettuce, onion for salad and radish.

Some half-season vegetables show a marked difference as to which half they give of their best in. For instance, broad beans, peas and early potatoes grow relatively poorly in the second half, from a summer sowing, when they suffer more diseases. In contrast, there is a large group which give reliable harvests *only* in the second half, because spring is their flowering season: these include bulb fennel, chervil, chicory, endive, land cress, turnips and oriental vegetables in general, including Chinese cabbage, mizuna, mustards, pak choi and tatsoi.

The plot is abundant in September, with many second plantings, including swede, purple sprouting broccoli, leaf radish, spinach, pak choi, chervil, coriander, endive and Chinese cabbage under fleece.

13

FEWER PESTS AND LESS DISEASE
ENCOURAGING HEALTHIER GROWTH

Continuing the theme of best sowing times, gardeners who make good choices about what to grow and when, while respecting the limitations of their plot and its climate and the time available, can avoid many potential pests and diseases to enjoy reasonably trouble-free growing. Never totally 'trouble free', though: we cannot expect nature to completely clear out the bits we don't like from certain areas. If slugs and snails are absent or, worse, poisoned, what are song thrushes to eat? If aphids are not allowed to establish in early spring, how can ladybirds feed and breed?

A healthy and happy garden comes from a balanced approach: from tolerating some pests and diseases, while at the same time keeping their *causes* to a minimum.

'Pest' is a value word: some of nature would use it of human beings. I use it here for insects, animals and diseases that damage our food plants. In the wider picture, these pests have important roles, such as recycling plant debris and clearing the garden of weak plants. To fit in with this, gardeners need to move the pendulum in the other direction and fill their plots with *healthy* plants which pests do not deem ready for recycling or removing.

Encourage health and balance

Soil is the engine room of healthy growth. Improving its quality by regular, balanced feeding, and through eliminating interferences such as digging, is a major step towards healthier plants.

Although this chapter looks at pests and problems, the underlying theme is actually health and bounty: how to achieve growth that resists potential problems. I urge you to see health as a positive state in itself, and pests and diseases as temporary occurrences when the state of health is disrupted.

Unfortunately, in both gardening and society as a whole, pests and disease are seen as invaders which need constant fighting off, often using synthetic and expensive materials. In fact, a gardener needs to offer protection to only a few vegetables at specific times, and many problems can be avoided by a sound approach, based on knowledge of potential difficulties before they occur.

Sometimes, what initially seems a problem is a perfectly natural and seasonal occurrence. For example, mildew on courgettes, squashes, cucumbers and pumpkins appears in the mild, moist conditions of autumn, when it actually aids plants to shed their leaves and their fruits to ripen, the only problem being if you want more courgettes, which are actually unripe fruits . . .

Cabbage white caterpillars on kale. The damage looks bad but healthy plants will recover.

More examples like these will become clear as you read on, and I hope you will come to enjoy a greater understanding of natural processes at work, and their purpose, however annoying they may seem at first acquaintance.

Golden rules

All pests have times of year when they are most numerous and active: aphids and flea beetles in spring, moths and midges in summer and autumn, red spider mite in warm, dry conditions, slugs in wet ones. Knowing each pest's preferences can help us avoid them overrunning our plants, chiefly by timing sowings to make plants' main growth happen when problems are less likely.

Below are some guidelines to always keep in the back of your mind when you are growing vegetables, with the aim of reducing damage. Remember that pests are almost always present, in small numbers we hope: otherwise their predators could not be.

Sow in the right season
The presence and impact of pests, or lack of them, is often a result of sowing and planting at a certain time. For example, leeks planted too late are at risk of suffering badly from leek moth; brassicas planted too early in the spring can be clobbered by flea beetles; and courgettes planted when it is too cold are often eaten by slugs. Growing healthy vegetables is a precise act: the dates suggested in chapters 11 and 12 aim to give best growth and fewest problems.

Sowing in the right season means plants encounter conditions in which they can achieve robust and often rapid growth, with fewer problems around them, as well as having more ability to grow away from any problems they meet. Compare runner beans sown in April, growing feebly and with slugs often eating any small leaves, with a later sowing in June when the extra warmth enables rapid growth, so that the very same slugs are barely interested.

Sometimes you can 'switch season' to avoid pests. If, for instance, your cabbage hearts are often holed by caterpillars, try growing spring cabbage sown in late summer, for harvesting in April and May, so avoiding the times when butterflies are on the wing. Where potato blight is a common problem, grow earlies instead of maincrop, so that they have done their growing before the arrival of midsummer blight.

Sow in the best conditions
For healthiest growth, give seeds and seedlings their favourite temperature and environment. These normally occur when you sow at the right time, but sometimes it also helps to sow seeds in a protected environment: seedlings in general are more vulnerable to pests than large plants, and certain seedlings have special difficulties. For instance, small leaves of beetroot are adored by birds and woodlice, so I advise sowing beetroot in modules under cover, for planting out when established; swede can be difficult to raise outdoors but grows well from an indoor sowing which affords protection against flea beetles eating its leaves.

Grow resistant plants
Sometimes there are varieties known to cope with certain problems that may be common

in your area. I have found that 'Grenoble Red' lettuces are less tempting to slugs than other varieties; red lettuces succumb to more mildew than green ones but suffer less from slug damage; savoy cabbages cope better with caterpillars than ballheads; and Sarpo potatoes resist blight well, although taste and texture are variable. On the other hand, I am not convinced by the performance of supposedly root-fly-resistant carrots!

Remember the following

- Check when susceptible vegetables may want covering with mesh or fleece.
- Growing suitable plants together, as recommended in chapter 12, creates more favourable growing conditions.
- Water less frequently and more thoroughly, to reduce slugs and fungal diseases.
- Keep grassy edges cut short, to reduce slug numbers.

Overwintered spring cabbage. There are no caterpillars in April and May.

Pests

Slugs and snails

I use the word 'slug' to embrace snails as well; most gardeners have to contend with both at some point. In my garden, on clay soil and in a damp climate, much of what I do is influenced by the need to keep their population at a manageable level. Since they are always present, or *potentially present*, I strive to reduce their likely habitats.

In dry conditions, slugs may not be a problem, but in warm, continually moist weather their numbers increase rapidly, and they forage more hungrily and further. Their favourite foods include salad leaves, brassicas, carrot seedlings and roots, potato tubers and beetroot. Some vegetables suffer little damage, alliums in particular.

The most eaten parts of a plant are the oldest and sometimes the most tender, rather than strongly growing, mid-plant leaves.

Slugs are most interested in outer leaves, which are decaying anyway.

> Slug habitats include weeds, old and decaying leaves, long grass, walls and piles of stone, and any spots which are consistently damp and dark.

Tidying the garden by removing older, decaying leaves is a good precaution.

Keep slugs away from tender seedlings in three ways:

- Sow each vegetable in its right season, so that young plants are strong enough to grow despite the occasional nibble.
- When sowing indoors, keep your propagating space clear of slug habitats and check any damp, dark spaces for slug arrivals.
- Sow outdoors in clean, bare soil, not close to overgrowing weeds or plants whose leaves are draping on to the soil. Slugs are another reason to keep weeds to an absolute minimum, to reduce damp habitats.

Any wet fortnight from about May to September can see slug numbers and activity increase dramatically. When this happens, it is worth venturing out at dusk or dawn with a torch to see exactly what is going on, and you may be surprised at their numbers. I take a pointed knife to skewer them, or you can put them into a bucket for later disposal – hens like snails above all.

Container plants are often vulnerable, with slug habitats nearby or underneath. A copper strip around the container can deter them, but make sure that no leaves are growing over it, providing an entry point. Hunt around your containers, especially

Slugs in salads can be reduced by frequent picking of small to medium-sized leaves, so that there are few if any larger leaves for slugs to live under. For more details, see chapter 14.

underneath any dark, damp objects, to remove lurking slugs.

Trapping slugs is effective but needs time, and in doing so you also catch centipedes and beetles. Deterrents such as soot, sand, gravel, salt and garlic need to be used with care – many plants do not like salty soil and too much gravel dilutes good soil and compost. Soot, sand and ash lose efficacy after rain.

'Organic' slug pellets of ferrophosphate are a milder poison. These are best used in moderation and kept for extreme conditions and the most vulnerable plants; likewise nematodes, which are effective but expensive, are wasted if the weather is dry after you apply them.

Caterpillars and flea beetles

These are common at particular times of year – flea beetles in spring and caterpillars in summer to early autumn – and mainly on brassicas. Often brassicas can be sown outside these times: for instance, rocket, mizuna and turnips in August rather than April. Or sow seeds indoors to protect seedlings and cover plants with mesh at planting time.

If plants outgrow the mesh towards the end of summer, butterflies are sure to arrive and you can squash their caterpillars if you find them, but this is impossible when they burrow into cabbage hearts and sometimes one is forced to admire their persistence, while trimming damaged leaves off hearts that you hope will be sound in the centre.

Leek moths

Leeks used to be one of the easier vegetables to grow, but a rapid increase of leek moth from France has necessitated new disciplines. The moth's caterpillars are small but they eat the plants' most tender leaves right in the middle, causing a severe reduction in growth and even the destruction of small leeks. For strategies against them, see page 187.

Leaf miners

You may never see a leaf miner but their eating is visible as pale yellow patches in otherwise healthy leaves. I put up with them as a minor nuisance of all the beet family, including spinach and chard, with most leaves healthy when soil is good.

A leek moth caterpillar in September.

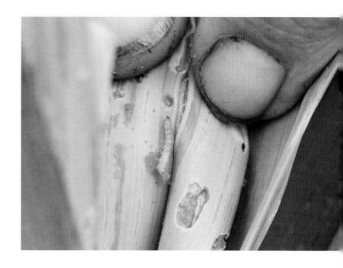

LEFT There are no root flies under the mesh. The carrot leaves push it up as they grow.

OPPOSITE LEFT Netting to prevent pigeons is best suspended above plants. RIGHT Pigeons have damaged this Brussels sprout plant, but the sprouts are still edible.

Root flies

Small and rarely seen, these can cause major losses when laying eggs on soil, for maggots to eat into roots, and the best remedy is a fleece or mesh cover. The two main ones are cabbage root flies, from April to August, affecting brassica plantings and radish, and carrot root flies in both early summer and autumn: see page 183.

Birds

Wood pigeons are usually the main bird problem; unfortunately they are becoming more tame and are now less easy to frighten away with compact discs, red bottles and the like. I find that the best protection is afforded by mesh on top of plants, or a net suspended above susceptible plants, chiefly brassicas in the winter half of a year. Birds' hunger varies with seasons and the weather: damage is most dramatic in cold winters, so be ready to cover plants if severe frost and snow is likely.

Plastic netting with about 2.5–5cm (1–2in) mesh – larger holes are better to let snow through – can be draped over stakes with upside-down plastic pots on top, or over large cloche hoops spaced at 1.2m (4ft) intervals. It needs to be held about 45cm (18in) above the plants so that pigeons cannot land on top and peck through the net.

Fleece can be used against pigeons in spring, for instance over early calabrese, cabbage and peas, when its warming effect is an extra benefit.

Rabbits

You will soon know if rabbits are present because plants disappear more rapidly and dramatically than from slug damage. Salads of all kinds, brassicas, some umbellifers and alliums are all at risk, most noticeably in winter and spring. Beds of susceptible plants can be covered with mesh, or the whole plot can be fenced, but this is tedious to install because you need either to bury it

to about 30cm (12in), or to run it over the soil surface outwards from the fence-line, for about 60cm (24in), to prevent rabbits digging underneath; grass can be allowed to grow through this and then be mown.

Mice and squirrels

Nibbling of roots and flower bulbs, or disappearing sweetcorn, pea and bean seed, suggest these animals, and there are no easy answers. Mice burrow out of harm's way and squirrels are too agile to catch: they even come into my barn and remove any hazelnuts they find.

Mice must and can be controlled, though, in a greenhouse, where you need to set traps whenever you have recently sown seeds; you may catch surprising numbers in search of food and shelter, and save your sowings of peas, sweetcorn and lettuce in the process.

Deer and badgers

The remedy for deer is expensive and time consuming – a 2.5m (8ft) metal mesh fence.

Otherwise their browsing can destroy many plants including beans, beets, salads and brassicas. Some netting as for birds may keep them out of particular crops.

Badgers also need a solid fence or wall to deter them, because they are hugely strong and surprisingly agile when attracted by the scent of almost-ripe sweetcorn, peas and strawberries. Most of the time badgers are more messy than destructive, but the ban on culling in Britain has resulted in soaring populations and it is now many years since I saw a hedgehog, one of their favourite foods. Unfortunately this has benefited the molluscs, because hedgehogs eat slugs.

Diseases

Blight

This common fungal disease, which affects both potatoes and tomatoes, is mutating and becoming ever more virulent, so that previously resistant potatoes such as 'Lady Balfour' are now suffering damage, and I know of no tomato varieties offering solid resistance. Spores of the fungi multiply on wet leaves when air is consistently humid *and* the mean temperature is above about 15°C/59°F for a week or more. Any spells of wet weather make blight likely from June onwards, when even indoor tomatoes can suffer if their leaves are splashed a few times during watering, especially in the damp air of early autumn.

Blight appears as brown patches on leaves, which make them translucent: see under 'Potato' and 'Tomato' in chapter 15. Infected plants, roots and fruits can be composted, even though the advice is often to burn them. This is necessary in North America, where a different strain of blight is able to survive in soil over winter. In Britain this does not happen, thankfully, so blight has to wait for its ideal conditions every summer and arrives only from June onwards, transmitted on spores in the air.

Some years are too dry for blight, but one does not know in advance. It makes sense, therefore, to grow more first and second early potatoes, which crop before blight usually arrives, and the resistant Sarpo varieties; and to grow tomatoes under cover, with careful watering to avoid wetting any leaves.

Damping off

This is another fungal disease of damp conditions, most harmful to tiny seedlings that are watered or rained on too often, are in soil or compost that is not sufficiently free draining, or are thickly sown, usually indoors: see chapter 10.

Onion mildew

A recent increase in this disease has caused

Blight on tomatoes, causing both leaves and stems to rot, and then the fruit.

much difficulty in both growing and storing onions. It starts as a grey mould on leaves in late spring, mostly in wet weather, and once established can cause leaves to yellow and growth to stop within two or three weeks. Bulbs are then small and stay infected with the mildew, which enters their neck in summer or autumn, causing a grey rot of the onion. Even bulbs that looked healthy at harvest may be infected.

There is no easy solution. Three tips are:

- Grow from seed rather than sets, as some sets are infected with spores of the mildew and this is difficult to recognize.
- Grow a resistant variety such as 'Santero' and 'Hylander'; more such varieties are being bred.
- Above all, do not sow or plant Japanese onions, except salad onions, in September, as they harbour the mildew through winter.

Other pests and diseases

Ants gathered in nests may secrete enough formic acid to damage roots and kill plants, chiefly when soil is warm and dry, so regular watering is a help; but ants have impressive persistence and in certain favoured spots they can become endemic.

Red spider mite is dangerous for aubergines and cucumbers, mostly under cover, where there is the warmth and dryness they need. Extra watering and frequently wetting plants' leaves should keep the mites under control. You can also buy predators every spring, but they are expensive and I have found that water is as effective.

Mildew is common on older leaves of many vegetables from about midsummer onwards, and is part of the growth process to allow space for the growth of new leaves. However, it may be troublesome in wet summers, especially on lettuce, and can partly be kept in check by regular picking of leaves. In my garden I grow endives in autumn, instead of lettuce, because they barely succumb to mildew and thrive in the shorter, cooler days, giving new harvests as late as November if it stays mild.

Onion with early stage white rot. White rot is highly damaging to alliums but relatively rare (see pages 186-7).

SALAD ALL YEAR ROUND
WHICH PLANTS TO GROW WHEN, AND HOW TO PICK THEIR LEAVES

Salad plants grow quickly and offer many meals, for less effort and in less space than many other vegetables. Here I describe how to grow a range of suitable plants for every time of year, with my special tips for growing them productively. (For advice on sowing and planting, see chapter 11.) It is possible to have leaves in all months: fewer in winter but of stronger flavour.

Within each season you can have a wide range of salad leaves, all with wonderfully different flavours. In winter, for instance, to go with the spicy leaves, such as mustard and rocket, which are easier to grow in the dark months than lettuce, there are many milder-flavoured salad leaves that you can harvest at the same time to balance the pungency, such as spinach, chervil, lamb's lettuce and winter purslane.

The changing possibilities of every season are a theme of this chapter, together with ideas for harvesting plants carefully in a way that prolongs their life. For example, each lettuce plant can yield a good number of leaves over ten to twelve weeks, which means that two sowings, in March or April and in June, can keep you in leaves for much of lettuce's outdoor season, from about May to early October.

Suggestions for growing and harvesting

Choosing which salads to grow

Flavours of home-grown leaves are richer and stronger than those of bought leaves, so check the 'Taste tips' on page 163. For healthiest plants and longest harvests, see the sowing dates given in the table on pages 166–7 and choose your plants for each season accordingly; sowing mizuna in March, for example, gives far fewer leaves than from an August sowing.

Plants for winter salad, photographed in October: lettuce, endive, leaf radish, coriander and mustards.

Proprietary seed mixes

You can either sow one of the mixes offered by many seed companies, or sow your own combination of seeds according to both what you like to eat and what is suitable for sowing at that time. While it is easier to buy and sow a mix, and probably cheaper on seed, better results come from a choice of individual seed packets, matched to their best months for sowing. One reason for this is that with commercial mixes of seeds and plants companies do not, in my experience, pay enough attention to seasonal needs. I feel it is worth paying more for individual packets of seed, to be sure of growing plants that are right for each season, and the extra cost of seed will be more than balanced by the longer harvests.

Sow direct or plant?

Either is possible, although for early spring harvests it helps to sow indoors at the dates given in chapter 11. Sowing direct may seem easier, but if you harvest by picking outer leaves of fewer, widely spaced individual plants (see below), rather than cutting thickly sown rows, you will need relatively few plants and therefore fewer sowings, so in fact sowing in trays, pots or modules and then planting out requires little or no extra time.

How many plants to grow

In fertile soil and compost, I find that fifty to eighty salad plants of different kinds (say lettuce, spinach, sorrel, dill in spring and endive, oriental leaves, lettuce, rocket in late summer) at a spacing of 22×22cm (9×9in) can give 1kg of leaves over about ten weeks in warm weather, outdoors and without protection. It is wise to grow a few extra plants to be sure of having enough leaves, in case there are any problems with pests or weather: sowing and/or pricking out into two module trays, of forty to sixty plants in each, should result in enough bountiful salad for most households. Alternatively, direct sowing of eight to twelve rows across a 1.2m (4ft) bed, with rows 25cm (10in) apart, can provide a similar harvest: thin plants after a month to allow15–20cm (6–8in) between them. If rows are left unthinned, plants live for a shorter period.

Where to grow

A shady area can work for salads as long as it does not stay damp all the time, which often results in damage from slugs (see page 152). All kinds of containers are possible (see page 164) – even on windowsills, in winter especially – because salads are shallow rooting, while bigger harvests over a longer period come from beds that include plenty of compost and well-rotted animal manure.

Feeding the soil for salad

Mature manures and composts are ideal for salad plants, offering a regular and accessible supply of small amounts of nutrients. The ability of organic matter to hold extra moisture is also valuable in growing consistent supplies of leaves, and helps plants to live longer. So before Christmas, spread your best compost or well-rotted manure, a year or more old, on the soil's surface. Using manure may sound odd if you are concerned about cleanliness, but soil needs lots of bacteria to grow healthy plants, and humans have evolved multiple resistance to bacteria as well as having millions of our own. Some commercial growers use cow manure for lettuce because it has an ability to confer on plants a resistance to fungal infections.

Sowing dates

Check my table on pages 166–7 to know the *most productive times* for different sowings. Sowings at the wrong dates give meagre pickings: mizuna, mustard and endive come up readily in April, make a few leaves and then rise to flower; spinach sown in May will flower early; lamb's lettuce sown in June and salad onions sown in July will be at risk of mildew. Sowing outside the times given is possible and sometimes unavoidable, but harvests will be smaller, over a shorter period and often less healthy.

LETTUCE FROM SOWING TO HARVEST

1 A selection of module-raised lettuce being planted in mid-June.

2 Three weeks later the lettuces are ready for a first pick.

3 The first pick: the outer leaves have been twisted off and any weeds removed.

4 Five weeks later, after several more picks, the lettuce are still growing.

Sowing direct

Salad seeds can be sown in shallow drills 1–2.5cm (½–1in) deep, and in dry conditions, moisten the soil or compost first, several times if really dry, and check with a trowel that moisture has penetrated at least 10cm (4in) below the surface. No extra water will then be needed for at least a fortnight. Lettuce may struggle to germinate in hot weather and can be started in shade indoors: scatter seed on moist compost in a tray and leave uncovered, with a sheet of glass on top to hold the moisture, and then prick out seedlings after about five days: see pages 108–9.

Watering

Salads need less frequent watering than is often realized, especially when there is compost to hold moisture. Soil and compost should look dry on top before you water. Water thoroughly every few days or weekly, instead of a sprinkling every day, which encourages slugs and mildew. Slow-growing winter salads need even less water.

Harvesting: size of leaves

You can allow leaves to grow as large as you like them, especially when you space plants 22cm (9in) apart. Leaf size varies with season – summer leaves are larger than winter leaves. Flavour tends to increase with both leaf size and the age of the plant. Thickly sown seedlings can be cut at the two-leaf stage, stems and all; called micro leaves, these are expensive and time consuming to produce, because harvests are small, with a need for frequent resowing, using plenty of seeds; this can be done at any time of year except midwinter.

How to pick leaves

Careful picking makes as much or more difference to the size and quality of harvest as does the effort put into growing plants in the first place. There are two options:

CUTTING If you allow plants to grow thickly in 25cm (10in) rows, say 2.5cm (1in) apart, the maximum harvest will probably be two or three cuts of all leaves, and you will need to grade out some of the yellowing lower leaves. Gather a handful of leaves and slice a knife horizontally just underneath your fingers, always cutting just *above* the smallest leaves you can see, not into the stem, so that regrowth is possible. Salads that regrow most quickly and healthily after cutting are chicory, endive, mizuna, mibuna, rocket, sorrel and winter purslane. Cutting is a useful way of tidying up an overgrown plant: first, cut out the healthy leaves; then you can cut and remove all older and yellowing leaves to allow a clean start, for easier picking next time.

PICKING OUTER LEAVES

1. Plant at a 22cm (9in) spacing.
2. Leave to grow until the plants' outer leaves are touching or nearly touching.
3. Gently twist or pinch off all larger leaves. On this first pick, a few of the outermost leaves are often somewhat damaged by slugs or disease – a one-off problem of the first pick: remove these leaves and compost.
4. Then after a week or so you can again pick the newly grown outer and larger leaves in this same way. The central, younger, smaller leaves keep growing into new harvests, every week during the growing season and for two or three months, with leaves in good health. For specific advice on picking, see 'Tips for each salad' on page 168.

How to pick hearts

Large, hearting plants need extra moisture, and are more prone to diseases that cause rotting of some heart leaves, so it is worth cutting the first hearts of each sowing of lettuce, endive and chicory before they are fully firm. This gives a week or more of harvests before plants are fully mature and decreases the risk of some hearts spoiling or flowering before you can eat them.

After cutting a heart out of lettuce, endive and chicory, more leaves appear from stems left in the soil. With endives in late summer, it is possible to cut almost-mature hearts just above the smallest leaves, gathering all leaves except the tiniest heart ones, and then have subsequent regrowth, even to hearting stage again.

Frequency of picking

In warm, bright weather growth is rapid and new leaves may be picked every five to seven days, compared with every two to four weeks in winter, when precious new growth is much helped by you picking rather than cutting leaves. In winter there are some salad plants such as mustards, rocket and mizuna which grow noticeably more quickly than others such as lamb's lettuce, chard and salad onion.

How to keep leaves fresh after harvest

Leaves are still alive after being picked and continue living for many days in cool dampness. To store them for later use, mix and wash in a container of cold water, drain the water out in a colander or spin it out, bag up any leaves that are not needed immediately and keep the bag in a fridge, or a cool but unfrozen outdoor space in winter. At temperatures between 2 and 10°C/36 and 50°F, bagged leaves will stay alive for up to a week, especially when they have been grown in healthy soil.

Taste tips

The bulk of most summer salad is usually provided by lettuce, whose flavour is rather mild and unremarkable, but with some distinctions. Leaves of most cos (romaine) varieties are sweeter; red varieties and leaves of flowering lettuce tend to be more bitter and sandy soils can also encourage bitterness. Lettuce hearts have probably the mildest and sweetest flavour of any salad leaf.

You can bring stronger flavour to summer salads by adding herbs such as dill, basil and sorrel. A small clump-forming type of sorrel called buckler-leaved is especially good for salads, with a refreshing, citric 'bite'. A wide range of basil varieties offer rich and diverse flavours, from strong lemon and lime to aniseed and mild cinnamon.

Flavours of many salad plants become stronger in autumn. On the one hand is the heat and spiciness of oriental leaves and rocket, and on the other is bitterness from leaves of endive and chicory, a great health tonic for the liver. Bitterness can be offset by the pungency of mustards and can be mitigated by allowing endive and chicory hearts to develop, also by blanching (see page 164) and using a sweetened salad dressing.

Winter salads can have the greatest range of flavour, because more plants are in season then than in summer, including herbs like chervil and coriander and strong-tasting leaves such as land cress.

For gentle heat in the salad bowl through autumn and winter, mizuna, pak choi and Chinese cabbage all have a nice balance of juiciness, crunch and mild pungency. Milder heat comes from leaves of young plants; then after two or three months' growth, leaves of some plants become extra spicy and hot, especially wild rocket and 'Green in the Snow' mustard. For a milder mustard try 'Red Frills', which also looks wonderful, both in the garden and on the plate.

Spinach has a flavour all its own, more agreeable than chard, and spinach leaves are noticeably sweet in late winter after frosts have helped some sugars to develop. Try chewing leaves thoroughly to let their flavours come out and fill your mouth, with a sweet aftertaste when plants have recently been frozen: the extra sweetness is a wonderful bonus in winter mustards, offsetting their piquancy.

163

Pests on salad leaves

Many salad leaves are tender and can be eaten in large quantity by pests: the potential for plenty of damage, at certain times in particular, means you need to be aware of how to avoid the dangerous moments.

Seasonal pests are lessened by sowing at the right time, which encourages stronger growth and enables plants to avoid the worst problems. Flea beetles on all young brassica leaves are a problem in the first half of the year – hence my advice to sow brassica salads after mid-July. Butterflies and moths on brassica leaves are another seasonal pest, in the second half of the year, but less damaging than flea beetles: if you want completely unholed leaves it is worth covering brassica salads with mesh or fleece in August and September.

Slugs are a potential problem at any damp time of year, especially from June to September. It helps to sow in season, and to harden plants off before setting out; also to keep weeds to a minimum and to remove yellowing older leaves, in order to reduce possible hiding places and to help the soil surface become dry after rain has cleared. For more details, see page 152.

Blanching

You can make leaves of large salads such as endives less bitter by depriving them of light for a week or two, by gathering them and tying with string, or by placing an upturned pot over the plants. However, this can cause some leaves to rot and encourage extra slugs: you may find it simpler to sweeten the salad dressing instead! Heart leaves are a form of self-blanching, as with chicory and endive sown in July.

Salad leaves in containers

Salads are an excellent vegetable for growing in small spaces and containers, with the potential for quick harvests of many flavours over a long period. For ideas on suitable containers see page 34.

Your own garden compost should be good to use when a year old and well broken down. Put some in a bucket first and pull out any woody pieces; then add some extra nutrients as for making a potting compost (see page 104). Multipurpose compost is easy to use and you can grow plenty of leaves in it before feeding becomes necessary. You can also grow good leaves in animal manure as long as it is dark and crumbly – a year old or more. Some of the illustrations show trays filled with cow manure and nothing else, but it may be better to mix it with some home-made or even green waste compost to dilute the richness.

Few plants are needed, so you could buy some: a mushroom crate of 30×40cm (12×16in) needs just six plants and a 25cm (10in) pot can have one or two. In larger containers I recommend the same spacing as in beds: an average of 22cm (9in) between plants, whether single or in clumps, carefully picked to prolong their lives.

After a couple of months, some outer leaves may show signs of yellow around their edges or have a hint of blue and purple among the green, showing that some feeding is necessary with a general-purpose liquid feed.

The need for water is often hard to judge because surface compost of outdoor containers, in damp but not really wet weather, can look wet on top and be bone dry underneath. When unsure, lift the container: sometimes you will find it surprisingly light and this means you need to water! Do so in gradual stages, every minute or so, allowing water to soak in rather than run through the dry compost.

Container salads in winter

Containers are especially useful in winter, as they can be brought indoors to encourage some growth of salads such as lettuce, endive, chicory, oriental leaves, spinach, winter purslane, land cress and salad onion. Placed on a windowsill through winter, turned fortnightly to give light to the other side, container-grown plants will produce a fair number of leaves from September sowings, until plants rise to flower in March and April – and the flowers are edible too.

Six September-sown mustard plants in a box in February – (left to right) 'Green in the Snow', 'Red Frills' and 'Pizzo'.

Salad plants to grow outdoors

The table overleaf has most of the information you need to grow good leaves of a wide range of plants. The 'best sow' column is most important for the chance of a long and successful harvest. Dates given are all for outdoor sowing, except basil, which needs the extra warmth and dryness of an indoor sowing.

Use this table to choose the leaves you most enjoy eating, and then draw up an approximate sowing plan.

Here is an outline of the main possibilities, from which you need only a few:

MARCH Sow first lettuce of different varieties (for leaves and/or for hearts), spinach, peas, salad onion, sorrel, orach, tree spinach, dill, flat-leaved parsley

MAY Sow chard or beetroot, chicory for forcing, basil

JUNE Sow second lettuce, kale, peas for shoots

JULY Sow chicory for hearts, summer purslane

LATE JULY Sow third lettuce, endive for hearts, wild rocket, spinach, Chinese cabbage, pak choi, tatsoi, chervil, coriander

EARLY AUGUST Sow any oriental leaves, salad rocket, endive, land cress

LATE AUGUST Sow lamb's lettuce (for winter), any oriental leaves, winter purslane, chicory for leaves

SEPTEMBER, FIRST WEEK ONLY Sow lamb's lettuce, mizuna, salad rocket, radish for leaves

PLANTS FOR SALAD LEAVES, sown and grown outdoors					
Salad (* = oriental leaves)	Family (see page 141)	Best sow	Harvest outdoor	Qualities	Tips
Basil	Mint	Apr–May in, Jun out	Jul–Sep	Big flavours, many choices	Keep plants warm and dry
Chard/leaf beet/ beetroot	Beet	Apr–Aug	May–Oct, Mar–Apr	Colours better than flavour	Pick small
Chicory, forcing	Lettuce	May–Jun	Nov–Dec, Jan–Apr	Yellow, crunchy	Force in darkness
Chicory, heart	Lettuce	Jun–25 Jul	Aug–Nov	Stores well	Fertile soil
Chicory, leaf	Lettuce	Jun–Aug	Jul–Apr	Winter hardy	Pick small
*Chinese cabbage, heart	Brassica	Jul	Sep–Nov	Crisp leaf, dense heart	Cover against insects
Coriander, chervil	Umbellifer	Jul–Aug	Sep–Apr	Winter hardy	'Calypso' coriander for a long harvest
Dill	Umbellifer	Mar–May	May–Jul	Early, fragrant	Sow in spring
Endive, heart	Lettuce	Jun–Jul	Sep–Nov	Large plants	Sow in summer
Endive, leaf	Lettuce	Jun–Aug	Jul–Apr	Disease free	Pick small
Kale, flat leaf	Brassica	Jun–Jul	Sep–May	Winter hardy	Spring flowers
*Komatsuna	Brassica	Aug	Sep–Nov	Fast, tender	Slug prone
Lamb's lettuce/ corn salad	Valerian	Aug	Oct–Apr	Hardiest salad plant	Sow direct in late August
Land cress	Brassica	Jul–Aug	Sep–Apr	Strong taste	Pigeon cover
Lettuce, heart	Lettuce	Mar–Jul	Jun–Oct	Sweet heart	Frequent sowing
Lettuce, leaf	Lettuce	Mar–Aug	May–Oct	Many harvests at 22cm (9in)	Pick outer leaves, no knife

PLANTS FOR SALAD LEAVES, sown and grown outdoors					
Salad (* = oriental leaves)	Family (see page 141)	Best sow	Harvest outdoor	Qualities	Tips
*Mizuna and mibuna	Brassica	Aug	Sep–Nov, Apr	Hardy, tasty	Many varieties
*Mustard	Brassica	Aug	Sep–Nov, Apr	Pungent flavour	Pick small, many colours
Onion, salad	Allium	Mar–Jun, end Aug	May–Sep Apr–May	Long harvest, hardy plants	Sow early or late
Orach	Beet	Feb–Apr	Apr–Jul	Vibrant colour	Avoid seeding
*Pak choi and tatsoi	Brassica	Jul–Aug	Aug–Nov	Varietal choices	Cover against insects
Parsley	Umbellifer	Mar–Jul	Jun–May	Long season	Flat or curled
Pea, for shoots	Legume	Mar–Jun	May–Aug	Rich pea flavour	Sow early for most shoots
Purslane, summer	Moss rose	Jun–Jul	Jul–Sep	Succulent	Needs dry weather
Purslane, winter	Claytonia	Aug	Oct–Apr	Hardy, tender	Cover from October
*Radish, leaf	Brassica	Aug–Sep	Sep–Nov	Abundant	Roots edible
Rocket, salad	Brassica	Aug	Sep–Apr	Hot flavour	Sow in Aug for healthy leaf
Rocket, wild	Brassica	Jul	Sep–Jun	Spring harvests	Wider spacing
Sorrel	Oxalis	Mar–Jul	Feb–Nov	Lemon taste	Buckler-leaved is good for salads
Spinach	Beet	Mar–Apr, Jul	Apr–Jun, Sep–May	Winter hardy	Remove slugs
Tree spinach	Beet	Mar–Apr	May–Sep	Colourful shoots	Pick shoots frequently

Tips for each salad

Basil

Grows best in full sun, under cover if possible, either in soil or in containers. There is a huge choice of differently flavoured varieties. To keep plants young and productive, pick leaves and stems regularly. Flowering shoots need to be removed as soon as they become apparent; and sweet basil (Genovese) is the most productive.

Chard and beets

These make leaves of great beauty, but when eaten raw the flavour is rather metallic and earthy, so they are best picked frequently as small leaves, and you probably need only one or two plants. Remove any flowering stems to prolong plants' lives over most of the

Chicory 'Castelfranco', with land cress (above) and Mizuna (below).

season, even through a mild winter and until the following May.

Chicory for forcing

Dig up its roots in late autumn, before Christmas at the latest, cut off all leaves for compost, and then pot on the roots in a bucket filled with any partly or fully rotted organic matter. Placing the bucket(s) in a dark cupboard at room temperature gives harvests of tight, yellow chicons within three to five weeks, and smaller second harvests after that, until April at the latest.

Chicory for hearting

Takes ten to twelve weeks from sowing. Avoid spring sowings, which risk flowering; sow from June to about the third week of July, and cut hearts as soon as they feel firm. Harvests in November can be stored somewhere cool and damp for salad leaves until January; also in November you can lift plants with a small root ball to store in a shed until needed.

Chicory for leaves

This is more bitter than chicons and hearted chicory but easier to grow, from sowings at any time in summer.

Chinese cabbage

Can be grown for leaves or heart, but it is highly susceptible to slugs and insects, so it is best to apply a mesh cover after planting; otherwise there will probably be caterpillars boring into the hearts in September and October. You can cut the hearts when either loose or firm, depending on how you like them.

Chervil

An autumn and winter salad of great delicacy and hardiness, with a flavour of mild aniseed. Sow and grow as for coriander below, but avoid spring sowings, which flower almost immediately.

Coriander

Often sown in spring and then flowers readily, although early spring sowings in March give more leaves than sowings in May. Sow the variety 'Calypso' in late July, for leafy plants through the autumn which may also survive the winter, to give leaves again in March and April and small umbels of tasty, pale white flowers in May.

Dill

A herb for spring and summer, best sown as early as possible, in February indoors or March outside, allowing time for plenty of leaves to grow and be picked before the plant's energies turn to flowering from late June and through the summer. The flower buds are edible but a little tough.

Endive for hearts

Endive comes in two main forms: either frisée with thin, serrated leaves, or scarole with thicker and larger leaves. Both can be sown from June to August, with the possibility of huge plants, but there comes a point where leaf quality deteriorates as the edges go brown, so it is best to cut out the hearts when they are of fair size and slightly blanched – to give you an idea, this is about ten weeks from sowing on average. After early autumn harvests, a second cut is possible.

Dill in early June, the stems elongating.

ENDIVE FOR LEAVES
The leaves are slightly bitter, from exceptionally long-lived, frost-hardy plants.
1. Sow in exactly the same way as endive for hearts, and using the same varieties.
2. Starting when plants are about six weeks old, twist and pick off outer leaves as needed. The first ones are often quite large.
3. Subsequent weekly pickings will be of smaller and prettier leaves, which should continue right through the autumn, from a sowing in late July or early August. Leaf endive, especially scarole such as 'Bubikopf', is a valuable leaf in November when early frosts have knocked back most lettuce.

Kale

Flat-leaved varieties of kale such as 'Sutherland' and 'Red Winter'/'Red Russian' have many possibilities, especially as salad at a time when leaves are otherwise scarce. Sow in June or July to grow large plants through summer and autumn, from which you can pick new small leaves and tender shoots from March to May.

Komatsuna

Also called mustard spinach, komatsuna is so fast growing that its tender leaves are easily holed by slugs. They have a pleasantly mild flavour and red komatsuna is attractive, similar in appearance to red pak choi.

Lamb's lettuce

Can be sown in spring, but in hot weather it may suffer from mildew and then flower. Best growth is in damper months, so sowings in August should result in healthier plants through autumn. Water them if the soil is dry in September and October. Sowings in late August are best for winter and early spring harvests: cut them when plants are about 7–10cm (3–4in) in diameter – a cold and fiddly job in winter. Cut a little higher than any visible rosettes coming out of the main stem to enable regrowth of smaller heads. You can increase the quality and size of winter harvests by covering plants with fleece from December.

Land cress

Flowers in spring and makes most leaves in autumn and winter, from a summer sowing. You can either cut across the top or pull larger leaves from around the edge. Plants are extremely winter hardy, but pigeons like them even more than we do and some bird cover is usually needed from about October.

Lettuce for hearting

For a few hearts at all times, sow monthly from March to June and then fortnightly in July. To spread the chances of always being able to harvest sweet, firm hearts, sow a few seeds of different varieties together, because they will mature at slightly different times: for instance, 'Little Gem' is earlier than 'Lobjoits'. Aim to cut hearts before they turn too pale and dense, because some leaves are prone to rot at that stage: browning at the edges of heart leaves (known as tipburn) is often caused by a shortage of moisture, so give extra water as hearts swell.

Lettuce for leaves

Can be sown as early as February indoors and from about the middle of March outdoors. See 'How to pick leaves' on page 162 for advice on spacing and I emphasize that how leaves are picked is the main influence on how plants grow and for how long. The other influence is having enough organic matter in and on soil, to hold plenty of moisture. The number of varieties available means a wide choice of flavour and colour: 'Bijou' and 'Rosemoor' for dark red leaves, 'Freckles' and 'Mottistone' for speckled colour – and the leaves of 'Freckles' are sweet, as are those of many green cos varieties such as 'Chartwell'. It is worth browsing through a catalogue or on the Internet (see page 200), bearing in mind that all varieties offered as hearting lettuce can be picked for leaves, in the way I describe. This significantly increases the choice of varieties for leaf lettuce!

Lettuce 'Amorina'.

Lettuce 'Bergamo'.

Lettuce 'Chartwell'.

Lettuce 'Freckles'.

Lettuce 'Mottistone'.

Lettuce 'Navara'.

Mizuna and mibuna

These are excellent salad plants, giving an abundance of slightly, but not over-spicy leaves. Good varieties of mizuna are 'Waido' F_1 for broader leaves with thicker stems, and 'Red Knight' F_1 for fewer but larger leaves with an attractive red colour. Larger leaves mean they can be picked individually, helping plants to live for longer; perhaps use a knife for cutting each leaf, to avoid rocking

171

Mizuna 'Red Knight' and mustards 'Green in the Snow' and 'Red Frills'.

growing. Spring sowing is best done during February indoors or March outdoors, until May. Sowings in early summer are at risk of catching mildew on their leaves when medium sized; they are best pulled if this happens, whatever their size.

Orach

This is a large plant but a minor addition to bowls of salad, for its dark red colour, as long as you can find seed of a crimson variety. Once you have a good plant, it is easy to allow seeding, but this may result in an orach weed problem. From June, or when 30–45cm (12–18in) high, plants make flowering stems in preference to leaves.

Pak choi and tatsoi

These are difficult to grow because of their extreme sensitivity to slugs. Sometimes one just has to accept a few holes in otherwise healthy, glossy leaves. I suggest carefully cutting larger leaves rather than slicing across the whole plant. Plants come in many shapes, colours and sizes; choose ones you like the look of. Red varieties of pak choi grow well and look great in salads. These plants are less winter hardy outdoors than other oriental leaves.

Parsley

Deserves to be more used in salads, for its excellent flavour and nutritious leaves with plenty of vitamin C. Flat-leaved varieties are most suitable and two sowings, in March and July, should give leaves for most of the year. Plants of a March sowing may grow right through until winter, but are more likely to flower at some point in summer. A summer sowing results in younger plants for winter with more chance of surviving frost.

the fragile roots. Plants survive a mild winter outdoors, with new harvests in March and April, followed by tasty flowering stems.

Mustard

Grows fast, resists much winter weather and is pungent. 'Green in the Snow' has the hottest and most frost-tolerant leaves, 'Pizzo' has crinkled green leaves and 'Red Giant' grows enormous leaves, better in stir-fries than salads. If I had to choose one variety it would be 'Red Frills', which looks stunning both in the garden and on the table, and grows leaves of a milder flavour.

Onions for salad

Onions can be sown in August to overwinter as small plants and, flimsy as they look, hardiness is assured. Growth in March and April will be steady and you can pull the plants at any stage, depending on how you like your onions. You can also pinch or cut leaves off and leave the plants

Peas for shoots

1. Choose seed of a tall variety, so that plants are vigorous.
2. Sow from March to June, in modules or direct, perhaps covered with fleece for a while to keep pigeons off. Be wary of sowing after June because pea plants in late summer and autumn are prone to mildew and also grow less before flowering.
3. When plants are about 30cm (12in) tall, cut or pinch off the top 5cm (2in) of stem, which will be delicious to eat along with its small leaves and tendrils.
4. Plants then look moribund for a few days before sending new shoots from many parts of the stem, as well as continuing to grow upwards, so another and more generous pick of shoots can be made after about ten or twelve days.
5. Keep picking all shoots weekly for another four to eight weeks, until new shoots become thin and many flowers appear; the flowers are edible too, or they can be left to make a few pods.

Purslane, summer

Thrives only in dry weather, but has lovely succulent leaves: sow in midsummer and hope for sunshine. To harvest, cut or pinch 2.5–5cm (1–2in) off its stems when about 15cm (6in) high, before the formation of any flower buds, which are difficult to see – small and of similar colour to the leaves, and with a bitter flavour. After the first cut, new stems will keep appearing out of the main one.

Purslane, winter

Thrives only in cool and damp weather.
1. Best sown in August for outdoor harvests and in September for harvesting through winter under cover, even a simple layer of fleece.
2. Start picking after about two months, when the leaves of clumps spaced at 20–25cm (8–10in) are touching, or when you first notice flower stems.
3. Clumps can be cut across the top or, much better, around their sides, for fortnightly harvests.
4. Main flowering happens in early spring: all the stems and flowering leaves can be eaten and look pretty in a bowl of mixed salad leaves. Unpicked flowers quickly form hundreds of seeds, which can be collected by pulling a whole plant, hanging it to dry and then rubbing out the tiny seeds. Some seeds are always dropped in the garden and this salad plant often becomes a weed.

Radish for leaves

Grows extremely fast in autumn. There is a mild taste of radish in the leaves, and if you do not pick them too hard you may also harvest a long white root of mooli radish by October. Plants survive moderate frost and can make it to Christmas if autumn is mild.

A salad of winter purslane and radicchio.

Rocket, salad

Best sown in early August for healthy leaves through autumn, possibly surviving winter too and giving a new flush of leaves and stems in March and April, by which time the plants will be eight months old. Picking larger leaves and removing yellow ones helps plants to live longer, but cutting is also possible. Many varieties are offered but I have always found the standard salad rocket to be the most reliable and tasty.

Rocket, wild

Grows well from being sown in July and allowed to make a fair-sized clump of leaves from plants at 20–25cm (8–10in) spacing. You can either pick outer leaves or cut across the top. Wild rocket often survives winter and can be cut again in April or early May, and then two or three more times at fortnightly intervals until there are too many flower stems after midsummer. Plants may survive for many years and become rather straggly, and they self-seed readily.

Sorrel

Easiest as a perennial, whose early spring leaves add a lemon flavour to a salad, until flower stems appear from May to July: keep snapping or cutting them off, until more leaves regrow through autumn and again in the spring. Roots can survive for many years and appreciate a mulch of compost in autumn. Broad-leaved sorrel is the most common variety: pick small leaves for salad or allow them to grow large for cooking in

Salad rocket in May – flowering and with flea-beetle holes in its leaves.

soups and omelettes. Buckler-leaved sorrel has smaller leaves which are tender and tasty in salad, but plants are more likely to die in winter than broad-leaved.

Spinach

Offers most leaves before and after midsummer, when it runs to seed. So a March or April sowing gives leaves for six to eight weeks; then a sowing in late July results in good-sized plants by mid-September and the possibility of leaves through autumn and again in spring, because spinach is impressively resistant to frost. Be ready for a few slug holes in the leaves, whose flavour should compensate for any ragged looks.

Tree spinach

Can be sown early, in February indoors or March to April outside. The tiny seeds are like the biblical mustard, growing into 1.5m (5ft) plants by the end of summer, and with harvestable shoots by May or June when plants are only 15–20cm high (6–8in). Pinch off the magenta-coloured growing point and then you can pinch off any other pretty side shoots – with just four or six baby leaves on each – on a regular basis; they have little flavour but look gorgeous, and new shoots keep appearing until early September on increasingly large plants, which then flower and set seed. One plant is enough for abundant harvests, and larger leaves can be picked for cooking.

Tender, colourful shoots of tree spinach can be picked frequently for salad.

15

A TOP TEN OF VEGETABLES
ACHIEVING LONGER, TASTIER HARVESTS

This chapter is to help you succeed with a few main vegetables: it adds cultural and harvesting tips to the important sowing and planting dates given in chapter 10.

Although there are just ten vegetables here, the knowledge of how to grow them opens the door to a great range of harvests, because of

- the number of different varieties available to try, for instance mangetout, sugar snap and normal peas, and a vast plethora of tomatoes
- the range of seasons in which they can crop, such as first early or maincrop potatoes, and broad beans overwintered or sown in spring
- the varied character of harvests from immature and mature plants, such as tender, pea-like broad beans and older, starchy ones
- the similar methods needed to grow other closely related vegetables, as with courgettes and summer squashes.

LEFT A cob of sweetcorn 'Sweet Nugget' F1 in August. There is a good combination here of tender sweetness and full-bodied kernels.
BELOW A carrot harvest of (left to right) 'Maestro', 'Honeysnax', 'Purple Haze' and 'Nantes'.

Broad beans

Broad beans in June, sown in early November. Three stems are growing from one seed, a process called tillering.

A hardy vegetable whose first harvests in June are an exciting, early taste of summer. Earliest harvests are from autumn sowing but overwintered plants are at some risk of succumbing to weather; see sowing tips below.

All beans have pink nodules on their roots, containing soil bacteria which help the leaves use nitrogen from the air, some of which is stored in the nodules and is then available to surrounding and following plants. Although they find much of their own nitrogen, broad beans still grow better in soil mulched with compost for moisture retention and plant health.

Sow/plant after

Autumn-sown broad beans can be started after many summer vegetables. Clear soil of any residues and weeds, dib holes 2.5–5cm (1–2in) deep for the bean seeds, and then cover all the soil with some compost or manure.

Sowing

Outdoor sowings in late October and early November are best covered with mesh, net or brushwood placed on top, to stop birds pulling them out when just shooting; or seeds can be sown in a greenhouse in mid- to late November, in 5cm (2in) modules or pots, for planting out in February. Spring sowings and plantings, from February to May outdoors, can be covered with fleece for four to six weeks to trap warmth as the sun rises higher. Although seed can be sown in June, plants crop less willingly in late summer and are often less healthy.

Cropping

FROM June, when sown in November.
UNTIL August, when sown in late April
and May.

Picking

Young pods can be eaten whole, as can the tops
of plants when they are in full flower, either in
salads or cooked as greens. Beans have different
flavours at all stages and you can rub the skins
off mature, starchy beans after immersing them
for a few minutes in boiling water, to leave a
dense, creamy kernel. Two or three weeks are
needed for tender, edible pods to mature into
dark green and brown pods with starchy beans,
and then another fortnight for pods to dry if
you want to keep some seeds.

Varieties

'Aquadulce Claudia' is best for overwintering
and has large, pale beans; 'Imperial Green
Longpod' has smaller beans of bright colour;
'The Sutton' makes more compact plants about
30–39cm tall (12–15in).

In containers

Tall bean plants are large for containers and
need support. 'The Sutton' is worth trying,
smaller and less demanding of water.

Needs

SOIL No special needs but overwintered beans
but prefer free-draining soils.
WEATHER Dry winters are better than wet
ones; spring frosts are not a problem but
severe winter frost may kill plants.
WATER Although beans are tolerant of drought,
watering in hot summer weather is beneficial,
mainly as pods start to grow and swell.
SPACING Having rows across beds, 39cm
(15in) apart, allows room to pick, with
10cm (4in) between plants.
SUPPORT of taller varieties is optional; I
don't, but it does keep beans off pathways:

run a string along sides of beds when plants
are about 75cm (30in) high, with stakes at
the corners
WEEDING Just keep soil clean as usual.

Possible problems

Black aphids clustering at the top of plants
in May and June are the worst potential
pests. Pinching off the tops to eat, when the
beans are in full flower, can prevent aphids by
depriving them of a landing place, because they
don't like landing on bare-topped stems; also
they are less common on the tougher stems
and leaves of autumn-sown plants. Otherwise
you can pinch off any aphid-covered top part of
plants (and compost) as soon as you see them.
A nasty disease is chocolate spot, a spreading
brown/orange fungus on leaves, most
common in poor soils and dry summers; giving
water helps if it is dry, as does boosting soil
fertility with compost for the following year's
beans. Mice can be a problem: pre-soaking the
seeds in water with a crushed clove of garlic,
overnight, can save them being eaten.

Tips

Broad beans freeze well and in a prolific year
they can give a serious amount of food.

Clearing/follow with

Cut stems at soil level with a spade or sharp
knife to leave the nitrogen-rich root nodules in
the soil for a following vegetable, which may
be any of leeks, calabrese, beetroot, salads –
depending when soil becomes clear. Chop bean
stems into 15cm (6in) lengths for composting.

French and runner beans

Runner bean 'Stenner' in August. The flowers suggest there are more beans to come.

These are the beans of summer, growing fast in warmth for regular picking. Dwarf beans are the first to harvest and also finish earlier; climbing beans are ready later, from about the middle of July and until September, but with less quality towards the end. A second sowing of climbing beans in late June will provide plentiful, top-quality harvests in early autumn.

Sow/plant after

Early beans can follow overwintered salads, cabbage and spinach, but often go into soil which has been bare since autumn. Planting is possible up to early July for dwarf beans

and these these later plantings grow well after carrots, beetroot, salads and garlic.

Sowing

Sow indoors early May and plant after mid-May, for earliest harvests. However, indoor sowing in May's second half for planting in June often works better, because these plants thrive in warm soil and are knocked back by any cold nights below 6–8°C/43–46°F. Outdoor sowings are most successful from early June.

Cropping

FROM early July, from dwarf bean plants sown indoors in early May.

UNTIL the middle of October, from sowings in late June.

Picking

In June and July there will be some lovely flowers, especially on runner beans, followed in as little as a week, on dwarf plants, by some rapidly elongating beans. You can choose whether to pick them young, small and tender, or larger and swollen. Regular picking of all beans before they swell with seeds helps to prolong the harvest. You can leave the pods of one plant unpicked to swell and then become dry, for sowing next year.

Varieties

Choices abound. My recommended dwarf bean variety is 'Cupidon', which offers plenty of long, green pods, and 'Sonesta' for good yields of yellow ones. Of the climbing French beans, 'Blue Lake' has small green pods, 'Blauhilde' purple; 'Borlotto' beans are mottled magenta on green, and succeed well as dried beans when left unpicked until late September, by which time their pods should be dry and hard with pretty beans inside, to store in jars and use as dry haricot beans.

Runner beans have either white or red flowers, or both, and were originally grown for ornament. I like 'Lady Di' (white flowers) and 'Enorma' (red flowers) for their long, stringless pods. 'The Czar' can be left unpicked to have an October harvest of large 'butter beans'.

In containers
Dwarf beans are a good vegetable for medium to large containers but watch for slugs nibbling them hard in wet summers. Runner bean 'Hestia' is compact and gives a fair crop from a large pot, without support.

Needs
SOIL Plenty of organic matter helps to hold moisture for these fast-growing plants – hence the method of filling trenches with compost, manure and organic wastes, and then re-covering with soil before planting climbing beans. An easier method is to mulch soil in autumn with 5cm (2in) of compost and manure, for planting beans into in early summer.

WEATHER Warmth is vital and some rain too.

WATER Be prepared to water thoroughly every four or five days in a dry summer, especially climbing beans. If you notice flowers falling off without setting beans, it means that plants need a good soak.

SPACING Space plants 30cm (12in) apart. Dwarf beans can be evenly spaced over a bed, while runner and climbing French beans may either be given a wigwam of 90cm (36in) diameter and six to eight plants with a cane each, or be grown in rows 30cm (12in) apart with space either side to walk and pick.

SUPPORT for climbing beans can be either bamboo of 2–2.7m (6–8ft) or hazel poles, pushed firmly into the soil and tied together at head height. Push supports into the soil when planting the beans, and then after two

or three weeks their fast-growing stems may need help to start twisting around the sticks.

WEEDING Pull any weeds you notice while picking and don't allow weeds to seed when partly hidden amongst the bean foliage – go looking for weeds and pull them when small.

Possible problems
Sowing and planting too early results in weak growth and slug-eaten plants with leaves more yellow than green. Lack of water is often an issue and the main reason for poor harvests in dry summers. Watch for slugs under dwarf beans and remove any you find while picking. Sparrows pecking red flowers of runner beans can be solved next year by growing a white-flowering variety such as 'Czar'.

Tips
The first planting of dwarf beans in mid-May can be covered with fleece for two or three weeks, to speed up establishment and bring the harvest forward a week or two.

Clearing/follow with
When the last beans are picked and leaves start to fall off climbing beans, you can remove them to compost; the stems are best cut or shredded to help them rot. As with broad beans there are nodules on the roots: many stay in the soil when the beans are pulled out, or you can cut the stems at ground level if you want to be sure of leaving all nodules in the ground.

Early dwarf beans can be followed with autumn salads, planted in late August or early September, and later beans can be followed with garlic if the soil is clear by early October. After clearing beds in early autumn, spread a light dressing of compost, to break down over winter and make soil ready for spring plantings of, for example, lettuce and brassicas, or sowings of carrots.

Carrots

Pulling carrots in June from a raised bed which I filled with mature compost the winter before.

Small carrot seeds are slow to grow and are often appreciated by slugs; if you come through that test, the carrot root fly awaits; if your carrots avoid them, you will enjoy a treat, because freshly pulled carrots are superior to anything you can buy.

Sow/plant after

First sowings for summer harvests need to be in completely bare soil where nothing has grown all winter. Mid-March is possible in a mild spring; early April is a good average time. Carrots sown in June, for autumn harvest and storing in winter, can follow early spinach and overwintered salads, or weeds – see below.

Sowing

Having clean soil pays off when sowing carrots because the tiny seedlings are so easily smothered by weed growth. If the soil is full of weed seeds, wait for some to germinate in April, and then hoe them off, two or three times at fortnightly intervals if there are masses; then sow carrots in June for winter use.

In clean soil, another option is to sow in June between garlic that is starting to go yellow as it matures. By the time you carefully remove the garlic bulbs with a trowel in late June, the carrot seedlings will be well established and ready for thinning to about 1cm (½in) apart, or twice that for larger roots.

Carrots can be sown in modules, or root trainers for longer depth of root: they must be planted as small seedlings, before the main tap root reaches the bottom. But sowing direct is the main method.

Cropping

FROM the third week of June, when sown by the middle of April.

UNTIL November, of large roots from a sowing in the middle of June, while later sowings until mid-July will grow smaller roots by late autumn.

Picking

When you can see the tops of small roots pushing up out of the soil, it is time to pull a few, perhaps with a trowel to loosen the soil at the same time as pulling gently. Early harvests from a few places along the rows help to make space for larger roots in another week or two; one sowing in April can then offer harvests throughout summer.

When harvested in October and November, for winter storage, carrots need to be separated into larger roots for later use (they keep better), and smaller roots for eating straight away.

Varieties

'Early Nantes' has round-ended roots and is excellent in any season, 'Autumn King' has pointed roots and good vigour for autumn harvest, 'Purple Haze' F_1 has great colour and 'Resistafly' F_1 is supposed to be disliked by carrot root flies – but I am not sure. All varieties can root into undug clay soil and I would resist the temptation to grow 'easy' round carrots, which do not give many meals.

In containers

Carrots are a good vegetable for container growing. Just be sure to thin them enough; otherwise you will have great leaves and small roots. Allow 5cm (2in) space for all roots after broadcasting seed.

Needs

SOIL All soils are possible, with some fine-quality compost on top, not dug in.

WEATHER Carrots do well in a wide range of temperatures; dry weather is good for increasing sweetness in roots.

WATER With summer sowings you may need to water in the bottom of drills before sowing the seed; otherwise be measly with the water to encourage sweetness.

SPACING Early sowings can be in rows as close as 15–20cm (6–8in) but otherwise 30cm (12in) rows are best, with roots no less than 1cm (½in) apart to allow growth of more roots, less leaves.

WEEDING is vital for carrot seedlings (see sowing tips above) and even when carrots are growing strongly, keep pulling any weeds you see to prevent them seeding.

Possible problems

Carrot root fly is the main issue, arriving in May and September, so all sowings are at risk of the maggots hatching in nearby soil and burrowing tunnels around the roots. You don't know they are there until the damage is happening, and roots can be inedible after two or three weeks of feeding by maggots. A remedy is to cover with mesh or fleece, from early May for spring crops and from August for autumn crops. Slugs like the leaves of seedlings and the taste of older roots: in clay soil, I suggest harvesting roots before the end of October. Slugs often graze leaves and roots in damp seasons.

Tips

Slug numbers are reduced by having nearby soil clear of weeds and other plants. Sowings in early April take about two weeks to become visible; if you can't see any, take a closer look and you may notice tiny stems of slug-grazed carrot, in which case you need to draw drills again for another sowing. Wet springs can see this happening more than once, while seedlings of carrots sown in dry conditions are most likely to succeed; after watering the drills before sowing, do not water for three weeks or so.

Clearing/follow with

Be sure to clear thoroughly all traces of carrot roots, to leave no homes for maggots. After harvests in June and July, soil can be given a light dressing of compost if none was given in the winter; then you can plant kale, dwarf French beans, beetroot and autumn salads. You can leave leaves of autumn harvests on the soil for worms to pull in, and spread a dressing of compost 2.5–5cm (1–2in) on top of them, after pulling any weeds.

Courgettes

Eight courgette plants in late spring, planted six weeks earlier, and garlic and lettuce behind.

Courgette plants grow fast and large, so be sure to allow room: up to 1m (39in) in diameter for each plant. In warm weather they can be highly productive and any unpicked courgette will soon grow into a marrow.

Sow/plant after

Best planted after soil has been bare for a good month, to lessen slug numbers. Or plant on a heap of half-ripe compost or manure.

Sowing

To enjoy harvests by midsummer's day, sow indoors around the third week of April, in 5cm (2in) pots: lay a seed flat on top of each, and then push in gently and cover with 1cm (½in) of compost. Plants can be set out when their

first true leaf has grown to a fair size, after about three weeks, and a covering of fleece will help them no end. Or you can move plants to a slightly larger pot and keep them indoors for an extra week. Handle plants carefully at every stage, because the roots, stems and leaves are all fragile.

Outdoor sowing needs the warmer soil of mid- to late May, until early June: place two seeds per station and thin to the strongest.

Cropping

FROM late June when planted around the middle of May, with a covering of fleece.

UNTIL either the first frosts in October, or earlier if mildew causes rotting of most leaves in cool, moist autumns.

Picking

First you will see exotic yellow flowers, some on stems (male) and some on fruit ends (female). Pick first fruits small, as short as 5–7cm (2–3in) long, because others will then develop better. By late July there should be a courgette every day or two, and you can choose your favourite size by picking or leaving them. Courgettes become marrows within a fortnight and growth of marrows slows development of new courgettes – see tips below.

Varieties

You can have long ones or round ones, green or yellow, although yellow fruiting plants are less productive than green fruiting ones.

In containers

One plant in a large container can produce worthwhile harvests but needs daily watering after the flowering stage, even if it rains, because the large leaves transpire a lot of moisture in all summer weather. Grow a small variety such as 'Bambino' F_1.

Needs

SOIL Courgettes need plenty of organic matter, either from spreading in winter or as a summer mulch around plants, to feed them and conserve moisture.

WEATHER Warm is best for healthier growth and plentiful pickings.

WATER It is worth watering in dry summers – a good soak every week – unless you have too many fruits: plants go semi-dormant in dry weather and become productive again after rain or watering.

SPACING 1m (39in) between plants.

SUPPORT is needed only in limited spaces: plants grow upwards until the stems gradually topple over in August, with new courgettes then growing close to the soil. To prevent that, you can tie stems gently to a stake, with a new tie every fortnight.

WEEDING Less is needed than for other vegetables because such large and fast-growing plants can smother weeds, but think ahead to next year's sowing and search even for hidden weeds, to pull them and prevent any seeding.

Possible problems

Slugs like young plants, especially when they are struggling to grow in cool conditions, so avoid setting out plants before mid-May. Cucumber mosaic virus can live in soil and cause healthy young plants to wither suddenly: if you suspect it, grow 'Defender' F_1, which has some resistance. Some lower leaves succumb to mildew as early as August and there is no remedy for it, but courgettes usually keep growing throughout September, even with white mildew on many older leaves.

Tips

Many leaves and stems have prickly spines, so gloves and a long-sleeved shirt may be useful for picking courgettes. Remove any sideshoots of new leaves on the lower stem; otherwise these grow marrows and prevent growth of courgettes at the main growing point.

Clearing/follow with

Plants can either be cleared to a compost heap in October or left to be killed by frost, whereupon they shrivel to a few fibrous remains and you can spread compost on top before Christmas.

I have sometimes planted garlic after clearing courgettes, but more often leave soil covered with compost through winter, then sow and plant a range of vegetables in spring.

Leeks

'Swiss Giant' leeks in late summer. They were sown in April and planted in June.

Growing leeks used to be straightforward until the leek moth became common. If you still don't suffer from it, count your blessings and enjoy harvesting a vegetable that resists slugs and frost and can be eaten from August to May.

Sow/plant after

Leeks can go into soil that has already grown early potatoes, overwintered broad beans or spinach. Be sure to water them in well and give some more water after a few days if it is dry.

Setting the roots of plants about 7cm (3in) below soil surface serves to blanch and sweeten the lower stem.

Sowing

Sow either in modules indoors from March, or around the middle of April in clean, fertile soil outdoors, to have plants of any size from knitting needle to pencil thickness by the middle of June. Clean soil is important because seedling growth is slow and baby leeks have fine, grass-like leaves that allow enough light to pass through for weed growth underneath. Sow in drills 30cm (12in) apart and with about two seeds per centimetre (four or five seeds per inch). One row across a bed can give at least forty good plants and when transplanting in June or early July, discard the small ones. If you suspect moth, seedbeds can be kept covered with fleece.

Cropping

FROM August for leeks of early, long-stemmed varieties such as 'Swiss Giant' and 'King Richard'.

UNTIL early May for the most frost-resistant, shorter varieties with darker leaves, such as 'Apollo', 'Bandit', 'Edison' and 'St Victor'.

Picking

Apart from summer varieties for early harvest, leeks are relatively slow growing and stand well. Gently pull larger leeks first, leaving their neighbours undisturbed: sometimes you may need to slide a knife or sharp trowel into the soil, around and underneath the roots, while pulling the stem. Trimmed roots and flag (leaves) can be left on the soil, as worms like to pull them in.

Varieties

See above under 'Cropping'. The faster-growing, long-stemmed summer varieties are vulnerable to frosts of about –4°C/25°F or colder, while those for overwintering are shorter and more hardy, finally reaching a good size in March and April.

If you sow only one packet and your winters are not too severe, the Autumn Mammoth varieties are top value because they grow large enough to pull in September, yet also have more resistance to midwinter frost than other autumn varieties, so should still be edible in April.

In containers

In a 30cm (12in) container you can grow a dozen leeks of good size if you are prepared to water regularly from about July, when the plants will be growing strongly; some feeding from about the middle of August will also help growth. I suggest growing early varieties or an Autumn Mammoth variety.

Needs

SOIL needs plenty of organic matter, especially for moisture retention.

WEATHER Summer warmth and moisture enable rapid growth, then after a dormant period in winter leeks grow again quite fast, until flowering in May.

WATER It is worth watering from July to September if soil becomes dry.

SPACING 15cm (6in) between plants or 10cm (4in) apart in rows 30cm (12in) wide.

WEEDING needs to be little and frequent, because leeks do not cover the soil and some weeds always grow; they are best removed when small – an easy job when there is compost on the surface.

Possible problems

Moths are not prevalent everywhere but if in your area, they can arrive at any time, mostly in August, to lay eggs inside the folds of small leek leaves, where the maggots can then eat baby leaves as they develop, and there is a risk of plants dying unless they are strong enough to keep producing more small leaves. So it helps to have sown and planted at the dates given above, in well-composted soil, allowing plants time to become well grown before the moths' main egg-laying time in August, and also to sow in modules indoors in case early moths find seedlings. To be almost sure of preventing damage you can lay mesh over the bed straight after planting, keeping it on until about mid-September, apart from removing briefly to weed.

Another problem can be white rot fungal mould of the roots (the same as on garlic and onions), which resides in pockets of infected soil for several years and is shown by plants suddenly yellowing as their roots turn to soft white mush. The only remedy is to grow elsewhere, but I have noticed a general decrease in white rot after years of surface mulching with animal manure.

Spots of orange rust are often present on leaves, mainly in dry soils that are low in organic matter. Rust slows growth but does not kill plants, and leeks grow out of it when soil is moist.

Tips

Leeks thrive in moisture, so regular watering in dry summers helps growth and reduces rust. You can earth up stems if you desire more white. Leeks can be harvested when frozen but if severe frost is forecast, it is worth pulling enough for two or three weeks and keeping them indoors, cool and not too frosty, with their outer leaves on, and then trimming and cleaning them before use.

Clearing/follow with

Harvests in August and September can be followed with autumn salads such as oriental leaves, and all debris needs to be removed before these are planted. Otherwise you can spread autumn and winter manure and compost on top of the leaves and by spring or early summer it should mostly have been taken in.

Onions and shallots

Six seeds of onion 'Red Baron' sown in a module gave four seedlings. They are shown here in early August.

These close relatives of leeks are great staples of the garden and kitchen but they are not always as easy to grow as used to be the case.

Sow/plant after

Clean soil is important because onion leaves offer no shading effect to discourage weeds. On the other hand, onions and shallots are slug resistant, so they can be grown in mulched ground where molluscs may be lurking.

Sowing

To grow from seed, sow in drills of clean soil in March, for transplanting by early May, or sow indoors from February to early March, in modules with six to eight seeds per cell to plant as a clump, which will grow into medium-sized bulbs.

For quicker growth, you may find it easier to buy onion sets/shallot bulbs for planting in March, not before mid-month or else they risk bolting. However, sets and bulbs sometimes bring an infection of mildew into the soil. This disease may also be increased by the presence of onions growing through winter, so I do not recommend sowing and planting seeds or sets of bulb onions in autumn.

Cropping

FROM July until early August.
STORES UNTIL following April or May, in dry, cool conditions.

Picking

Wait until about half the leaves have fallen over, in early July for shallots and by mid-August at the latest for onions; then pull all bulbs, with their main roots, and leave them on the soil for a few days to dry in the sun and wind. When they are partly dry you can collect them up and spread them out under cover, with the leaves still on and some air around them, to finish drying; or plait or bunch them and hang in an airy spot. Once they are dry, and if not infected with mildew, onions and shallots should store throughout winter, either indoors or in a shed, even if it is frosty.

Varieties

There is a wide choice of red and yellow onions and shallots; try a few and see which you like. If mildew is a problem, try 'Santero' and 'Hylander' onions (both F_1s), which resist the disease.

In containers

The value of these vegetables compared to the cost involved makes them marginal for containers, but salad onions are worthwhile: see chapter 14.

Needs

SOIL being clean of weed seeds is helpful, and good onions grow especially well in undug soil with a mulch of compost.

WEATHER is most critical in June and July, when warm sun helps growth and then drying.

WATER is rarely needed but will make a difference if spring is really dry.

SPACING is variable: closer spacing gives smaller bulbs but does not spoil results. Modules with three or four onions or shallots in each, planted at 25cm (10in) apart, give medium-sized bulbs; sets need about 12cm (5in) each way or plant 7cm (3in) apart in 25cm (10in) rows.

WEEDING Hoe in April when weed seedlings are just visible and again in May before onion leaves are in the way; then hand weed every two or three weeks. Keeping the soil clean will allow you to make a rapid sowing of oriental leaves, turnips, etc. into clean soil afterwards in August: see chapter 6.

Possible problems

White rot infects onions, as for leeks above. The larvae of onion fly occasionally chew into leaves of all alliums in May and June, but damage is rarely significant. Mildew (neck rot) is a more dangerous problem: see pages 156–7.

Tips

Red onions are the most difficult to grow, especially from sets, which often bolt, unless you grow the more expensive heat-treated sets, which are available in early April. Growing from seed is worthwhile for red onions. Shallot bulbs can be replanted every year without buying new ones. Set aside some smaller ones at harvest time: small bulbs grow clumps with fewer shallots which then grow larger. Growing from seed is more economical than growing from sets and I have enjoyed huge harvests from one standard-sized packet, in relatively small areas of rich soil, from multi-sown modules planted at the spacings suggested here.

Clearing/follow with

After removing bulbs and clearing any weeds, sow or plant straightaway, any of oriental leaves, rocket, endive, chicory, turnip, winter radish, lamb's lettuce, land cress and winter purslane.

Peas

Tall yellow and purple peas growing up tripods of hazel poles in June.

Pea plants vary from self-supporting bushes to tall vines needing support. Some peas mature and finish early, others crop later, some have edible pods either with peas or without (sugar snap and mangetout respectively): see varieties below. Whatever variety you choose, the sweetness and juiciness of freshly picked peas are a joy.

Sow/plant after

Peas are best sown in spring, either where soil has been bare through winter for sowings in March and April, or after overwintered brassicas, leeks and salads for later sowings in May.

Sowing

Mice and birds love pea seed, so it is worth sowing indoors in modules from mid-March to early May, with a mousetrap near by, to have small transplants ready after two or three weeks: sow two or three seeds per cell and plant as a mini clump. Or sow seed outdoors from April to mid-May, covering seeds and plants with fleece until they need support. Later sowing is possible, but quality and yield will be lower. Sowing in November to have small plants through winter and an early crop in spring is often recommended, but I have never succeeded in bringing a worthwhile number of plants to fruition.

Cropping

FROM June for first early varieties sown in March and April.

UNTIL August from May sowings.

Picking

Soon after flowering you will see baby pods and about a fortnight later these will swell with peas. Pick at any stage according to whether you want small, sweet peas or larger, starchy ones. If you want to save seed, leave one or two plants unpicked and pick the pods when brown and dry two or three weeks after the main harvest is finished.

Varieties

Always check a variety's height -to be sure of having the ones you want. Round-seeded varieties such as 'Feltham First' are early to crop, but with less sweetness than wrinkle-seeded varieties such as 'Greenshaft' (bush), 'Alderman' (tall), 'Mr Bray' (tall heritage) and 'Tall Sugar Snap'. I prefer sugar snaps to mangetouts for their sweetness: sugar snaps are picked when pods are full, whereas if you grow mangetouts, they need to be picked before peas are much developed, as otherwise the pods become stringy. There are also varieties with blue and yellow flowers and pods which mostly look better than they taste or yield. If you want peas in late summer, from sowing in June, try a mildew-resistant variety such as 'Oasis', but I find it still succumbs to some mildew and yield is poor.

In containers

Bush peas grow well in containers and can be followed with autumn salads. Slugs need controlling as they like pea pods.

Needs

SOIL can be enriched with extra organic matter on top, because peas love compost mulches for their ability to hold extra moisture.

WEATHER is likely to be best for peas in the spring – mild or warm and with some moisture in the air, rather than hot and dry.

WATER is often needed, especially for tall varieties, which consume large amounts.

SPACING depends on variety grown: 10–15cm (4–6in) between plants and 60–150cm (24–60in) between rows – less for bush varieties and more for tall ones.

SUPPORT of varied sizes, according to the variety grown, can be with hazel branches or poles, or netting. Peas can be grown up wigwams, spaced as for climbing beans, but with some string meshed around the sticks in a cobweb fashion, for tendrils to hang on to.

WEEDING is easy when peas are well supported, by hoeing along the edge of a row and a little hand weeding among the plants.

Possible problems

Once your plants have grown away from mice, birds and slugs, there is little to fear until the arrival of pea moth and mildew in July. I know of no remedy, and neither problem is catastrophic, but early sowings do better for mostly avoiding them. There is a risk of pigeons stripping leaves in spring; if this happens, you need to grow bush varieties, which can be covered all the time with fleece or mesh.

Tips

Peas for picking shoots to eat in salad are grown without support and closer together: see page 173. Sweet peas can be sown and grown as for tall peas, only a few plants being needed for many pickings.

Clearing/follow with

Remove all stems and old leaves as soon as you have picked the last pods, giving time for many second plantings such as beetroot, kale and leeks after peas finishing by late June. Later harvests of peas can be followed by sowings or plantings of autumn and winter salads, spinach, spring cabbage and spring onions.

Potatoes

'Charlotte' potatoes of one plant in mid-July, grown in manure on a surface of mulched grass.

Early potatoes are one of the first new vegetables to be ready in June, even in May if late frosts are absent. The flavour of freshly harvested tubers is especially fine and varies interestingly according to variety.

Plant after

Potatoes are the only vegetable I know which like mechanically loosened soil, so I often grow them after parsnips, whose harvest causes loosening to some degree, as one levers the soil to remove them. On top of that, potato plants thrive in some extra compost or manure, both as food for the hungry plants and to provide a loose medium in which the tubers can swell more easily.

Planting

Potatoes do not have to be chitted (sprouted), but if you buy tubers a long time before planting them it is worth spreading them in a box near some light, to prevent the growth of long, pale sprouts. Then use a trowel to place tubers 5cm (2in) below soil level in late March for earlies, and during April for others, even into the first week of May.

Summer plantings in order to have new potatoes for Christmas succeed with difficulty because of the prevalence of blight in late summer and autumn: see below.

Earthing up

Pull soil up around the stems as plants grow, to support them and prevent greening of the tubers. Augment the ridging effect by spreading organic matter around plants. If you use unrotted material such as grass and straw, slugs will tend to increase and may damage the tubers. I like to use part or well-rotted manure and compost, and then level it off after the harvest to grow leeks and autumn salads.

Cropping

FROM late May for first earlies, as soon as leaves show some yellowing.

UNTIL September for maincrops, best harvested by month's end, before slugs cause damage to tubers.

Harvesting

You can remove a few potatoes by feeling around in the soil underneath from mid-May onwards, leaving the plants to continue growing. Biggest harvests will be from plants that have had time to arrive at the point of maturity with leaves turning yellow and brown, but blight may force an earlier harvest: see 'Possible problems' below. Most no-dig potatoes can be gathered after loosening them by simply pulling the main stems, then use a trowel to check for a few deeply bedded ones.

Varieties

First earlies are more about speed than exquisite flavour, but just having fresh potatoes in May and June makes them worthwhile. Also, along with many second earlies, they crop before the arrival of potato blight, so a harvest is assured, although there is some risk of frost damage to leaves in May. Choose the variety that suits your dates and culinary needs. My favourite is a second early, 'Charlotte', for yield, good taste and keeping quality; I also grow a salad potato such as 'Pink Fir Apple'. The Sarpo varieties are resistant to blight, but their flavour is not remarkable and they have a dry texture.

In containers

Potatoes grow well in containers, buckets and sacks, but yields may be lower than is sometimes claimed, and tall-growing leaves can be invasive. A cheap method is to buy a 40-litre sack of multipurpose compost, cut the top off, make a few small drainage holes in its sides and bottom, and remove about a third of the compost. Plant your seed potato 10cm (4in) deep in the remaining compost; then after four to six weeks, when growth is becoming exuberant, re-fill the sack with the compost you removed at planting time. When the leaves start to yellow, pull them out and tip the sack into a wheelbarrow to harvest the potatoes; you can spread the compost around vegetables or keep it for later use.

Needs

SOIL is best reasonably loose, and/or with a thick mulch of organic matter.

WEATHER The ideal for potatoes is for emerging leaves not to encounter frost in April and May (cover with pots or earth up as much as possible if frost is forecast), and then without continual dampness after mid-June, when blight can otherwise become established.

WATER is worth giving to large plants when flower buds appear and in dry conditions generally.

SPACING is closer for early potatoes, at 30–40cm (12–16in), than for maincrop, at 40–50cm (16–20in), between plants.

WEEDING is mostly through a smothering effect when earthing up or spreading compost, but do remove all other weeds as potatoes are growing.

Possible problems

Blight is a major disease which kills all leaves, probably infecting tubers as well, when there is a week or more of rain and dampness from late June, and in any other wet period until autumn. First signs are some pale brown patches on leaves, which can cover the whole plant within a few days, unless sunshine returns. To prevent blight damage of tubers – showing as brown patches, which quickly spread and cause smelly rotting – it is worth cutting all stems and composting them once you notice the first infection; then harvest tubers on the next dry day.

Tips

Dry conditions are best for harvesting potatoes to store; otherwise spread them on dry soil or staging, where their skins can dry before you put them in sacks, and then keep somewhere dry and cool. If there has been blight on leaves, some tubers may be infected and rot later in store, so it is better to eat these quickly. Green potatoes are mildly poisonous, but a slight greening on one side can be cut off before cooking; when potatoes are stored through a mild winter, some sprouts will grow out of them and need rubbing off before peeling.

Clearing/follow with

Remove all leaves and compost them, including any with blight. Early potatoes harvested in June can be followed by plantings of leeks and French beans, or sowings and plantings of any second vegetable listed in chapter 12. Harvests of second earlies and maincrops in August or later can be followed with autumn and winter salads.

Sweetcorn

Sweetcorn 'Sweet Nugget' F1 in September, showing wonderful development of kernels.

This is really worth growing at home for the exquisite sweetness and taste of freshly harvested cobs. You can harvest them at whatever stage you prefer: young and milky or older, sweeter and denser.

Sow/plant after

Best sown and planted in bare soil that was composted in autumn or winter.

Sowing

Sweetcorn needs warmth. In much of Britain this means sowing outdoors in late May or early June, which gives only just enough time for cobs to mature, except in a hot summer. Reliable harvests come from sowing indoors after mid-April, to plant out from early May, and a fleece cover will help these plantings until early June, unless it is unusually warm.

Cropping

FROM August for early varieties in a warm summer.

UNTIL October for later varieties and in cool summers.

Tips for picking

When the cobs' tassels are turning dark brown, the kernels will be mature and should be both sweet and full. If you pick earlier the kernels will be smaller and of a paler colour; if you pick later the kernels will be dark yellow with less sugar and more starch – mealies.

Varieties

Choices cover flavour, height of plants and maturity dates. I find 'Sweet Nugget' F_1 is reliable and delicious, of mid-season maturity. You can also grow mini corn varieties but they take a lot of room, for little harvest, and if left to grow larger the cobs are not especially sweet or full.

In containers

Sweetcorn plants are large and benefit from a long root run, so are not ideal for container growing, and need plenty of water.

Needs

SOIL needs to be moisture-retentive and with a mulch of compost on top.

WEATHER Sweetcorn needs warmth throughout, with some moisture in summer.

WATER Watering is beneficial if the soil is really dry in August and early September.

SPACING An even spacing of 30–39cm (12–15in), for example in four rows along a 1.2m (4ft) bed, allows pollen to fall from flowers in summer and to drop evenly on the cobs' tassels, making for a full complement of kernels.

SUPPORT is not necessary for the strong, woody stems.

WEEDING is needed around and under sweetcorn with some hoeing and hand weeding, even in summer when the plants are tall and vigorous, to prevent any seeding.

Possible problems

In Britain there are few pests, although slugs sometimes eat early sowings when plants are struggling to grow in cool soil, shown by yellow leaves. As cobs ripen, badgers and birds become interested – hopefully only the latter because there is no remedy for badgers except a minimum 1.2m (4ft) wall or sturdy fence.

Tips

Sweetcorn plants, raised in small pots, can be planted between trailing squashes in late May and early June. In a 1.2m (4ft) bed, I grow two rows of widely spaced sweetcorn plants, 1m (39in) apart on either side of the bed and between the squash plants, also planted 1m apart: see illustration on page 140. Sweetcorn also grows well between 2m (6½ft)-high espaliered apples in my orchard. Plants are smaller than in open soil but cobs still develop full sets of kernels.

Clearing/follow with

Cut surface roots with a knife or sharp spade, and chop the stems into 15cm (6in) lengths before composting. If you clear them before mid-September there will be time to plant autumn salads such as rocket and mizuna, or you could plant garlic and broad beans in October.

Tomatoes

'Sungold' tomatoes in a polytunnel in September, grown in soil that was manured but not fed.

Growing tomatoes at home allows you to choose from an exciting range of flavours, colours and fruit size. In Britain, however, an outdoor harvest is rarely assured: tomatoes need warmth and dry leaves, so when it rains enough in summer to cause blight, all is lost. For wetter areas in the north and west, I suggest growing tomatoes under cover.

Plant after

Tomato plants are slug tolerant but a mulch of dark compost helps meet their need for warm soil . There is scarcely time for a preceding harvest in spring outdoors, but in a polytunnel they can follow winter salads, which may finish on the same day that you plant the tomatoes.

Sowing

Sow indoors in late February or March, first in a seed tray or small modules; then pot on the plants after a month or so, to have 20–30cm (8–12in) high plants by May for indoor planting, and by early June for outdoor planting. It is good if plants have their first truss of flower buds just developing at planting time.

Cropping

FROM late June indoors, for early varieties such as 'Sungold'.

UNTIL October, when all remaining, fully grown fruit are best picked to finish ripening in the warmth of a house.

Picking

The change from first colouration to full ripeness of fruit can take a maddeningly long time, between one and two weeks, but is worth the wait. Tomatoes taste best when at least three-quarters coloured, but become soft and a little bland if left on the plant after becoming fully ripe.

Varieties

Choice of variety is important. First decide which kind and size of plant to grow:
- a bush variety at soil level
- a tumbling variety for hanging baskets
- a determinate (cordon) variety for staking and training, up to 2m (6½ft) or more.

Then have a look at all the fruit options – cherry for sweetness, plum for cooking, normal size for yield, or beef for texture and flavour. Different hybrid varieties are offered every year, some with excellent flavour, or you can grow old-fashioned varieties from which it is possible to keep your own seeds.

I suggest in a first year of growing tomatoes that you buy one plant each of many different varieties to try them out (see page 200), rather than sowing lots of seeds all the same.

In containers

Tomatoes, of the bush or trailing types, are excellent in containers. Cordon tomatoes can be grown in large containers or grow bags, and need weekly feeding from July to September and almost daily watering.

Needs

SOIL A 5–7cm (2–3in) dressing of animal manure can provide enough nutrients for sustained growth, without any liquid feeding: a rich and moisture-retentive soil shows its qualities when growing tomatoes.

WEATHER needs to be warm and avoid planting too early, because an unexpected spring frost after planting early tomatoes may kill them.

WATER is needed by the roots and not on leaves, so *water the soil or container only*. I water twice weekly in hot weather, but containers often need daily watering in sunny weather and when plants are large.

SPACING You can space at 45cm (18in) but 60cm (24in) allows better growth and more room to pick fruit, remove weeds and prune plants.

SUPPORT is needed for cordon plants: either a cane or stout stick, with plant stems tied loosely to it at intervals of about 20cm (8in). Or in polytunnels use a string, with one end in the planting hole (placed there when planting) and its top tied to the structure above: twist the plants around it as they grow, while the string becomes held securely in the soil by tomato roots enveloping it.

WEEDING Keep looking for weeds under bush plants, even though the plants are good at covering the soil, and hoe between cordons.

Pruning

Cordon plants need side shooting at planting time and weekly thereafter: remove each new stem (shoot) that grows out of the main stem, just above where each main leaf joins the main stem. Cordons need their main growing point removed in August, to encourage ripening of existing fruit rather than formation of more young tomatoes. Likewise, pinch out all growing points of bush tomatoes through August and September.

Possible problems

Blight is the number one problem, with the potential to spread quickly, as on potato leaves. If this happens during a short, wet week, you can pass quickly from keen enjoyment and anticipation to a ruined harvest. To avoid it indoors, always be careful to water soil and compost only, and it is best to remove the lowest couple of leaves in July, allowing you to water without wetting leaves. Don't open roof lights in greenhouses if there are tomato plants underneath, because any rain on leaves will allow blight to develop, and once inside a structure it spreads to all plants, slowly in dry air and faster in moist weather.

Nematodes in soil that has grown tomatoes for several years can hamper growth, but plants will fruit well nonetheless. After experimenting with expensive, grafted plants that boast resistance to nematodes, I feel that soil pests pose less of a threat than sometimes suggested, unless you are a commercial grower of long-season tomatoes every year. Also I find that the exuberant growth of grafted plants can delay ripening of fruit.

Tips

Less water is needed by September and you can stop watering indoors altogether from mid-September, to encourage ripening and increase the sweetness of the tomatoes.

Clearing/follow with

Outdoor plants will finish in October unless blight has curtailed them earlier, in which case clear them to the compost heap, and there may still be time to sow and plant some autumn salads.

Indoor tomatoes, removed in mid-October, can be followed straightaway by plantings of all kinds of salad, which need to have been sown in about the middle of September. They require no extra compost or manure if tomatoes and other summer vegetables had the recommended amount, a little of which will probably still be on the surface when planting salads in October. Tread the soil down before planting, to break up any lumps and make it level, and water thoroughly.

AFTERWORD: FANCY GOING FURTHER?

This is a brief look at further, exciting ways of achieving healthier, more bountiful harvests.

Working with the moon

There are so many possibilities, according to whether the moon is waxing or waning, ascending or descending, and in which constellation it resides. But which of these has more importance?

Gardening by the moon is something that almost everybody practises differently and I hesitate to offer precise advice. On the other hand it is a fascinating subject and a great way to become familiar with less visible influences on growth.

Carrots 'Early Nantes'

In September 2009 I made a bed of 1.2 × 2.4m (4 × 8ft), by filling a wooden frame with well-rotted cow manure on top of grass and surfacing it with a 3cm (1in) layer of fine compost. I grew salads in it that autumn.

In April I measured the bed and divided it into two equal halves, A and B, and sowed carrots 'Early Nantes', to compare moon days given in Maria Thun's calendar:

A was sown on a 'bad' day, 12 April (dashed lines, sow nothing).
B was sown on a 'root' day with the moon in Taurus, 19 April.

It was a dry spring, I watered occasionally, and there was no carrot root fly.

Harvests were as below, with a first weighing on 29 July of one row from each half:

	A	B	
29 July	1.6	1.8	
12 August	1.8	2.4	
26 August	1.9	2.3	more forked roots in A
2 September	2.4	2.6	last rows, similar quality
Total	**7.7kg**	**9.1kg**	

Summary: 20 per cent more roots on an earth day sowing, although it was a week later. The quality of roots was mostly similar.

Moon carrots, 2 September: those sown on a 'bad' sowing day on the left, those sown on a 'root' sowing day on the right.

I have done a few moon experiments, of variable outcome. They mostly demonstrate an influence, but less predictably than I understand. Opposite are the results of one in which I sowed carrots on two different days, deemed suitable and unsuitable in Maria Thun's calendar (see page 200).

Maria Thun's advice concentrates mainly on constellations in which the moon resides at the time of sowing, rather than moon phases such as waxing and waning.

Other research has pointed to more vigorous growth of plants sown when the moon is waxing, especially in the few days before a full moon: see my book *Salad Leaves For All Seasons*, page 58. In the experiment above, 12 April was a waning moon and 19 April was waxing, so perhaps this had an effect.

Biodynamics

Using the biodynamic preparations is another exciting way to achieve better harvests. I give only a brief mention here and suggest you visit the website of the Biodynamic Agricultural Association (see page 200).

I use the soil preparation 500, which involves an hour of vigorous stirring to mix it with water, before flicking it on the garden in early spring and late autumn. I feel that soil is much enlivened by it and my gardens are healthy, but I have no way of proving a link between one and the other.

Farmers who use the preparations on a much larger scale report impressive changes to their soils and many more worms.

There are also biodynamic preparations for enlivening compost heaps and helping them to decompose more healthily. And for many other aspects of gardening.

But I notice that biodynamic gardeners are often keen on digging, even double digging.

Nobody has all the answers!

I hope you enjoy using the different ideas and methods presented in this book, to create a way of gardening that works for you.

SUPPLIERS AND RESOURCES

FERRYMAN POLYTUNNELS LTD, Bridge Road, Lapford, Crediton, Devon EX17 6AE (www.ferryman-polytunnels.co.uk) sells a wide range of polytunnels in widths of 2.4–7.3m (8–24ft), lengths in any multiple of 1.5m (5ft) and heights of 2.1–3m (7–10ft).

HIGH-QUALITY COPPER TOOLS can be found at www.implementations.co.uk, PO Box 2568, Nuneaton, CV10 9YR.

LBS HORTICULTURE LTD, Standroyd Mill, Cottontree, Colne, Lancs BB8 7BW (www.lbsbuyersguide.co.uk) carries a wide and good value range of useful accessories, including netting, mesh, fleece, plug/ module trays and polytunnels.

OSMO OIL AND PAINT, all of natural materials, gives excellent protection to the wood of raised beds and greenhouses: Unit 24, Anglo Business Park, Smeaton Close, Aylesbury HP19 8UP (www.osmouk.com).
A different branch of OSMO makes organic fertilizers and soil improvers, listed at www.osmo-organics.co.uk.

CHASE ORGANICS LTD, Riverdene, Molesey Road, Hersham, KT12 4RG (www. organiccatalogue.com) for seeds, gardening aids, comfrey roots, etc.

ORGANIC COMPOST for plant raising from West Riding Organics Ltd, Halifax Road, Littleborough, Lancs OL15 0LF (www.wrorganics.co.uk).

PLUG AND MODULE TRAYS are much harder to buy than should be the case. B&Q sell sturdy plastic ones, good for several uses (www.diy.com).

ORGANIC PLANTS from Delfland Nurseries, Benwick Road, Doddington, March PE15 0TU (www.organicplants.co.uk): an excellent range and with good advice.

FOR AN EXCELLENT CHOICE OF SCYTHES, try Simon Fairlie, Monkton Wyld Court, Charmouth, Bridport DT6 6DQ (www. thescytheshop.co.uk).

BIODYNAMIC AGRICULTURAL ASSOCIATION, Painswick Inn, Gloucester Street, Stroud GL5 1QG (www.biodynamic.org.uk) for information and supply of preparations.

BOOKS

Maria and Matthias Thun, *The Biodynamic Sowing and Planting Calendar*, Floris Books, published annually

Charles Dowding, *Organic Gardening: The Natural No-Dig Way*, Green Books (second edition, 2010)

Charles Dowding, *Salad Leaves For All Seasons*, Green Books (2008)

Charles Dowding, *How to Grow Winter Vegetables*, Green Books (2011)

WWW.CHARLESDOWDING.CO.UK has much information on vegetable growing, no-dig and, of course, Charles's courses!

INDEX

Page numbers in **bold** indicate where the main information about a vegetable will be found. Page numbers in *italic* refer to illustrations.

ACKNOWLEDGMENTS

A big thank-you to the many people who have helped create this book, ranging from the editors and staff at Frances Lincoln to participants on my courses, whose feedback is so interesting and helpful, and above all my family, who are keenly aware that I am so often in the garden, or writing about it, and support me in being rather single-minded!

In another sense, I am so grateful to the soil and plants which put up with all my experiments and then reveal some of their preferences and potentials. In the process they have enabled the creation of a really beautiful garden. Looking ahead, I am sure there is a great deal more to be discovered, understood and appreciated, through trying new methods and then from close observation of the results.

On which note I acknowledge you, dear reader, for using and then developing the methods and ideas of this book, to discover a more bountiful future.